ACQUAINTANCE AND DATE RAPE

Recent Titles in
Bibliographies and Indexes in Women's Studies

Immigrant Women in the United States: A Selectively Annotated Multidisciplinary Bibliography
Donna Gabaccia, compiler

Women and the Literature of the Seventeenth Century: An Annotated Bibliography Based on Wing's *Short Title Catalogue*
Hilda Smith and Susan Cardinale, compilers

Women and Mass Communications: An International Annotated Bibliography
John A. Lent

Sources on the History of Women's Magazines, 1792–1960: An Annotated Bibliography
Mary Ellen Zuckerman, compiler

Feminist Research Methods: An Annotated Bibliography
Connie Miller with Corinna Treitel

War and Peace through Women's Eyes: A Selective Bibliography of Twentieth-Century American Women's Fiction
Susanne Carter

American Women Playwrights, 1900–1930: A Checklist
Frances Diodato Bzowski, compiler

Women in Japanese Society: An Annotated Bibliography of Selected English Language Materials
Kristina Ruth Huber, with Kathryn Sparling

United States Government Documents on Women, 1800–1990: A Comprehensive Bibliography, Volume I: Social Issues
Mary Ellen Huls

United States Government Documents on Women, 1800–1990: A Comprehensive Bibliography, Volume II: Labor
Mary Ellen Huls

Mothers and Daughters in American Short Fiction: An Annotated Bibliography of Twentieth-Century Women's Literature
Susanne Carter, compiler

Women and Work in Developing Countries: An Annotated Bibliography
Parvin Ghorayshi, compiler

ACQUAINTANCE AND DATE RAPE

An Annotated Bibliography

Compiled by
Sally K. Ward,
Jennifer Dziuba-Leatherman,
Jane Gerard Stapleton,
and Carrie L. Yodanis

Bibliographies and Indexes in Women's Studies, Number 21

GREENWOOD PRESS
Westport, Connecticut • London

Library of Congress Cataloging-in-Publication Data

Acquaintance and date rape : an annotated bibliography / compiled by Sally K. Ward . . . [et al.].
p. cm.—(Bibliographies and indexes in women's studies, ISSN 0742–6941; no. 21)
Includes bibliographical references and indexes.
ISBN 0–313–29149–7 (alk. paper)
1. Acquaintance rape—United States—Bibliography. 2. Acquaintance rape—Bibliography. 3. Rape—United States—Bibliography. 4. Rape—Bibliography. I. Ward, Sally K. II. Series.
Z5703.4.R35A28 1994
[HV6561]
016.36288′3—dc20 94–21870

British Library Cataloguing in Publication Data is available.

Library of Congress Catalog Card Number: 94–21870
ISBN: 0–313–29149–7
ISSN: 0742–6941

First published in 1994

Greenwood Press, 88 Post Road West, Westport, CT 06881
An imprint of Greenwood Publishing Group, Inc.

Printed in the United States of America

The paper used in this book complies with the Permanent Paper Standard issued by the National Information Standards Organization (Z39.48–1984).

10 9 8 7 6 5 4 3 2 1

CONTENTS

ACKNOWLEDGMENTS

This work grew out of our interests in and concern about acquaintance rape on college campuses. For several years we have worked on the problem--as researchers, students, teachers, and service providers. Along the way, many people have contributed to the current work. Kathy Chapman was the project manager for a study of acquaintance rape on our campus, and part of her work involved an extensive search of the literature in 1988. We are grateful for her thorough and thoughtful efforts. Susan Ault was a member of the project team after the data were collected, and she added to the literature search in several ways, most especially in terms of her vast computer expertise. Ellen Cohn, Susan White, and Kirk Williams, were faculty colleagues and co-investigators with Ward on the study at the University of New Hampshire, and their contributions were numerous. Ronet Bachman worked on the project during the transition from the incidence study we conducted to the current bibliography, and her careful reading and creative ideas about research needs were invaluable. Jay Fraser helped extensively as the bibliography project has neared completion, and we are grateful to him for finding those last few hard-to-locate articles.

We hope that this bibliography is a useful tool for others who attempt to add to the knowledge about acquaintance and date rape and for those who work with the many victims.

ACQUAINTANCE AND DATE RAPE

1

INTRODUCTION AND OVERVIEW OF THE BIBLIOGRAPHY

Acquaintance rape has received a great deal of attention from scholars over the past several years. It is now acknowledged that this is a distinct type of sexual assault, and that it is a significant social problem and a common occurrence, especially on college campuses. Much scholarly work has been published, yet there is no one source of bibliographic information on this work. This bibliography catalogs works on date and acquaintance rape that have been published in recent years, primarily since 1980, but occasionally earlier.

Acquaintance rape is defined here as sexual assault that occurs when the victim and perpetrator know each other through some form of accepted social contact. This includes everything from a first meeting at a college party to a marital relationship. Date rape is sexual assault that occurs when the victim and the perpetrator are involved in a dating relationship, ranging from the first date to a steady dating relationship. The distinguishing characteristic of date and acquaintance rape, then, is the socially defined and accepted nature of the relationship between the victim and the perpetrator.

This bibliography includes scholarly works on acquaintance rape, based on this definition. Prior to about 1982, the term "acquaintance rape" was rare. Terms such as "dating violence," "dating assault," and "male sex aggression in dating relations" had been used in the literature, but it wasn't until the publication of a large-scale, scientific study by Mary Koss that the term "acquaintance rape" became an important conceptual category in the field. It is fairly straightforward to identify relevant works since the diffusion of the term acquaintance rape, but prior to this, there is some question about what works in the extensive rape literature would be appropriate for inclusion. We have followed several rules to make the selections incorporated in this bibliography. First, research had begun to show that the majority of sexual assaults were committed by perpetrators known to the victim (e.g., Ageton 1983; Sorenson et al. 1987). We have included studies that made a contribution to the conclusion that the prevalence of rapes involving prior victim-offender relationships called for a separate categorization of this type of assault.

Second, if a work deals with sexual aggression or assault in dating relationships, it is included regardless of the particular label used. Thus, the work of Eugene Kanin on male aggression is included (Kanin 1957, 1965, 1967a, 1967b, 1969, 1971; Kanin and Parcell 1977; Kirkpatrick and Kanin 1957).

Third, if a work became important in the development of the concept of "acquaintance rape" it is included here even if it did not deal specifically with sexual aggression in dating relationships. A good example is the work of Neil Malamuth on rape proclivity among college men (Malamuth 1981, 1986; Malamuth and Check 1980; Malamuth, Haber, and Feshbach 1980; Malamuth, Heim, and Feshbach 1980). Malamuth and his colleagues carried out extensive research on the population of college males and their responses to rape depictions and their self-acknowledged likelihood to rape. Later work which was crucial in the development of the concept of acquaintance rape also concentrated on the college population and placed sexual assault within the parameters of "normal" behavior; the work of Malamuth and colleagues was vital to this development, so it is included here.

Finally, within the research literature on rape, there was a growing emphasis on the relationship between victim and offender. In particular, researchers questioned the effect of prior relationship on perceptions about what constitutes rape, and the way such incidents are handled by authorities. For example, the work on the victim-offender relationship had begun to show that if the victim knew her attacker, then the rape label was less likely to be applied by societal observers, including authorities responsible for dealing with the crime of rape. The work of Martha Burt, for instance, had established that rape myths were common, and some of these myths involved the relationship between the victim and the perpetrator (Burt 1980; Burt and Estep 1981; Burt and Albin 1981). We have included work on rape myths since several of the important myths deal with the victim-offender relationship. An additional type of work included is research on the response to assaults when the victim and offender are acquaintances, especially the response of the criminal justice system. A good example is the study of rape victims by McCahill, Meyer, and Fischman (1979) which provided evidence that the criminal justice system responds differently when the victim and perpetrator know one another and that the recovery process for the victim is different if she knows the attacker.

Of course, we have tried to include all of the work that specifically deals with "acquaintance rape" and "date rape," once those categories became common in the literature. There is a final selection criterion that we have used, even for the literature specific to acquaintance rape. That is, we have included only works that are scholarly or scientific, as opposed to popular press or opinion pieces. Much has been written about acquaintance rape in the popular press, but our interest is in developing a tool for researchers rather than to study popular opinions about the phenomenon of acquaintance rape. So, for example, "op-ed" pieces and personal statements about acquaintance rape like that of Katie Roiphe (The Morning After 1993) are excluded from this bibliography. To be included, a work must be empirical research or a review of research, published in a scholarly journal or book form.

The works included have been organized into several topical areas, each of which forms a chapter of the bibliography. Many studies include more than one topic, and we have attempted to cross-reference works in the index. We have also provided an alphabetical listing of the works included at the end of this introductory chapter; the number after each reference indicates its chapter, and sequence within the chapter, to aid in locating the annotation.

The annotations include a brief statement of the purpose of the work, the method used to make the empirical observations, where appropriate, and an overview of the findings of the research. The remainder of this chapter is devoted to a brief summary of each chapter.

INCIDENCE OF ACQUAINTANCE RAPE

The vast majority of the work on the incidence of acquaintance rape has been conducted on college campuses. As early as 1957, sexual aggression research was being completed on campuses, and since the nationwide study by Mary Koss (1987, 1988), there have been many studies on different campuses. Although many of the studies use the instrument developed by Koss (Sexual Experiences Survey), others do not, so there is some inconsistency in the definition of terms. Nonetheless, the research indicates that acquaintance rape or attempted rape is a common occurrence; the estimate from the Koss study is that 25% of college women have experienced attempted or completed rape by an acquaintance since the age of 14. Other studies find similarly high incidence rates. The specific figures are reported in each annotation.

SOCIAL CORRELATES OF ACQUAINTANCE RAPE

Three types of studies are included in the category of social correlates of acquaintance rape. First, much research has substantiated the link between alcohol (and drug) use and acquaintance rape. Such aggression is more likely to occur when the victim and/or the perpetrator have been drinking. The perception is that sexual experiences that occur in conjunction with alcohol use are less serious and less likely to be considered as rape than are unwanted experiences that occur in the absence of drinking. The research on these links is presented under the social correlates category.

A second type of research we included under social correlates is the research on victim characteristics. Research on victims of stranger rape has found few consistent patterns of characteristics that victims have in common. However, since acquaintance rape is linked with a social context that, by definition, connects victim and perpetrator, it may be possible to identify patterns of victim characteristics for this type of sexual assault. This is not to argue that a victim is to blame for her victimization, but, rather, that there is some pattern in the social context within which victimization takes place that might be manipulable to decrease the likelihood of victimization. Examples of such research are studies of dating behavior, sexual activity, childhood sexual abuse, and interaction skills.

Most research on acquaintance rape examines women as victims and men as perpetrators. This is the most common form of victimization. However, there is some evidence that males can also be the victims in such incidents. The social correlates research includes a few examples of research on male victims of acquaintance rape.

Other categories of social correlates research include research on the link between attitudes and acquaintance rape, self-esteem and victimization, and other social correlates.

MISPERCEPTIONS OF SEXUAL INTENT

Because acquaintance and date rape occur within socially sanctioned relationships, the phenomenon of the perception and misperception of sexual cues is relevant. This is an important way in which stranger and acquaintance rape differ. A growing body of research examines these misperceptions, using experimental and survey methods. The research shows, in general, that men are more likely to interpret friendly behavior in sexual terms, while women see the same behavior and cues as nonsexual. The differences in perceptions may account for the frequency of acquaintance rape in otherwise "normal" situations.

RESEARCH ON PERPETRATORS

Two types of studies are included as research on perpetrators. First, there is a body of research on men (usually) who self-identify as aggressors in sexual situations. These men are labelled actual perpetrators here. A second group, also included in this chapter, is the group of men who indicate the likelihood that they would be sexually aggressive in varying situations. These are considered potential perpetrators, and this research deals with their proclivity to rape. This research has shown that men who admit to sexually aggressive behavior tend to accept rape myths; they are more traditional in their gender role expectations; and they are more accepting of interpersonal violence than their nonaggressive counterparts. But a significant finding of this research is the general similarity between those who acknowledge aggression and those who do not. This has been taken as evidence of the "normality" of the acquaintance rapist or potential rapist.

THEORETICAL PERSPECTIVES

Definitional issues and possible theoretical explanations are included here. Because acquaintance rape is a conceptually distinct category, questions of definition are still being worked out in the literature. Several studies of the definitional issues are included here.

A variety of theoretical perspectives has been used to try to explain acquaintance rape. These include social learning theory, feminist theory, social support, innate characteristics, ethnomethodology, economic inequality theory, and sex role socialization. There have been efforts to develop particular theories to explain acquaintance and date rape, and these efforts are included here. Particularly noteworthy is the theoretical work of Shotland, who tries to develop a theory to differentiate between different types of date rape, dependent on the stage of dating (Shotland 1985, 1989, 1992).

ATTITUDES TOWARD ACQUAINTANCE RAPE

A great deal of research covers issues of the attitudes of the public, especially the college student public, toward acquaintance and date rape. There is a great diversity of opinion about what constitutes rape, and this is especially the case for acquaintance situations. Studies of cultural beliefs, rape supportive beliefs, variations in interpretations depending on the behavior of the victim and perpetrator, sex role stereotyping, the effects of force and resistance on definitions of the situation, and similar issues are included in this chapter. There is a diversity of research and findings, as the annotations illustrate.

ATTRIBUTIONS OF RESPONSIBILITY FOR ACQUAINTANCE RAPE

A subset of the research on attitudes is the research on attributions of responsibility and how these attributions are affected by subject characteristics, such as gender, and by characteristics of a hypothetical acquaintance rape situation. These studies are presented in a separate section since there is a tradition of attribution research, particularly in psychology, that led to the application of attribution theory to the case of rape and acquaintance rape. Variables that have been shown to be important in this research are gender, with males being more likely to blame the victim; attitudes toward women, with those having more traditional attitudes more likely to attribute blame to the victim; and sex role attitudes, the more traditional being more likely to blame the victim. The sexual behavior of the victim has also been shown to be important, and in situations where the victim willingly engaged in some sexual foreplay, she is more likely to be held responsible for the eventual unwanted sexual aggression. There are gaps in this research literature that are identified by the studies reviewed.

LEGAL ISSUES

Acquaintance rape presents unique problems for the legal handling of such cases since the victim and offender are involved in some sort of social relationship. These legal issues are dealt with by the several studies included in this chapter. Of particular importance are the studies of the reform of rape laws to include issues of acquaintance rape and the studies of and research on the handling of such cases by the judicial mechanisms on college campuses.

CAMPUS RAPE

As indicated above, the vast majority of studies of acquaintance rape have been carried out on college campuses. In fact, the research is so disproportionate that there is a wide gap in the literature on community settings. Most of the research on campus rape finds its place in some other chapter in this bibliography, particularly in the incidence chapter, the attitudes chapter, or the attribution chapter. There are some studies that deal with a range of campus-wide issues that are included in this chapter, however. The chapter on campus rape includes a listing of the additional research on campus rape that is presented elsewhere in the bibliography.

MARITAL RAPE

There are several examples of research on marital rape that are included here. Marital rape represents an extreme of the continuum that constitutes the category of "acquaintance". Marital rape was not even considered a possibility until the rape law reforms began to eliminate the marital exclusion in recent years. It is a special case of acquaintance rape that has unique elements that are reviewed in the research presented in this chapter.

GANG RAPE

There has been relatively little research on gang rape where the victim knows her assailants. What research has been done has focused on gang rape on college campuses. The role of fraternities and athletic teams in gang rape is explored in the studies included here. The factors associated with acquaintance rape perpetration--attitudes toward women, adversarial sexual beliefs, rape myth acceptance--are also important for gang rape. But in addition, there is the role of the dynamics of all-male groups that create situations conducive to gang rape on campuses.

TREATMENT OF VICTIMS AND PERPETRATORS

Because acquaintance rape is different in important ways from stranger rape, the experience of victims differs. Research on the differences is included here. Victims of acquaintance rape are even more reluctant to report their victimization to authorities than are victims of stranger rape, and this delay in reporting creates additional recovery problems for them. Policies and procedures to deal with victims and to prosecute perpetrators are evolving on college campuses. These are reviewed in several of the selections in this chapter. One area that is identified for future research is the evaluation of the policies and procedures that have been developed. Very little is known about what works and what doesn't.

PREVENTION PROGRAMS

Just as college campuses are developing policies for dealing with cases of acquaintance rape, they are also developing programs, particularly educational programs, to prevent acquaintance rape. Several studies of the various efforts to prevent acquaintance rape are included here. This includes research on avoidance strategies, deterrence of acquaintance rape, and recommendations for colleges that are trying to develop programs.

Again, as with treatment programs, much more research is needed, as indicated in several of the citations here, on the evaluation of what constitutes an effective prevention program.

BIBLIOGRAPHY

Each study listed in this bibliography is included in one of the chapters described above. As an aid in searching through this literature, the works are listed below in alphabetical order. The number following each entry indicates the chapter and sequence in the chapter for the annotation. To find a particular work identified in the alphabetical list, turn to the chapter indicated by the first part of the number and then locate the reference in the sequential order given by the second part of the number. For example, reference 2.14 would be annotation number 14 in chapter 2.

Abbey, Antonia
1982 "Sex Differences in Attributions for Friendly Behavior: Do Males Misperceive Females' Friendliness?" Journal of Personality and Social Psychology 42,5:830-838. [4.1]

Abbey, Antonia
1987 "Misperceptions of Friendly Behavior as Sexual Interest: A Survey of Naturally Occurring Incidents." Psychology of Women Quarterly 11:173-194. [4.2]

Abbey, Antonia
1987 "Perceptions of Personal Avoidability Versus Responsibility: How Do They Differ?" Basic and Applied Social Psychology 8,1&2:3-19. [8.1]

Abbey, Antonia
1991 "Acquaintance Rape and Alcohol Consumption on College Campuses: How Are They Linked?" Journal of American College Health 39,4:165-69. [3.1]

Abbey, Antonia
1991 "Misperception as an Antecedent of Acquaintance Rape: A Consequence of Ambiguity in Communication Between Women and Men." Pp. 96-112 in Acquaintance Rape: The Hidden Crime, edited by Andrea Parrot and Laurie Bechhofer. New York: John Wiley and Sons. [4.3]

Abbey, Antonia; Catherine Cozzarelli; Kimberly McLaughlin; and Richard Harnish
1987 "The Effects of Clothing and Dyad Sex Composition on Perceptions of Sexual Intent: Do Women and Men Evaluate These Cues Differently?" Journal of Applied Social Psychology 17,2:108-126. [4.4]

Abbey, Antonia and Christian Melby
1986 "The Effects of Nonverbal Cues on Gender Differences in Perceptions of Sexual Intent." Sex Roles 15:283-298. [4.5]

Acock, Alan C. and Nancy K. Ireland
1983 "Attribution of Blame in Rape Cases: The Impact of Norm Violation, Gender and Sex Role Attitude." Sex Roles 9,2:179-193. [8.2]

Ageton, Suzanne S.
1983 Sexual Assault Among Adolescents. Lexington, MA: Lexington Books. [2.1]

Aizenman, Marta and Georgette Kelley
1988 "The Incidence of Violence and Acquaintance Rape in Dating Relationships Among College Men and Women." Journal of College Student Development 29:305-311. [2.2]

Amick, Angelynne E. and Karen S. Calhoun
1987 "Resistance to Sexual Aggression: Personality, Attitudinal, and Situational Factors." Archives of Sexual Behavior 16,2:153-163. [2.3]

Bachman, Ronet; Raymond Paternoster; and Sally Ward
1992 "The Rationality of Sexual Offending: Testing a Deterrence/Rational Choice Conception of Sexual Assault." Law & Society Review 26,2:343-372. [14.1]

Barbaree, H. E.; W. L. Marshall; and E. Yates
1983 "Alcohol Intoxication and Deviant Sexual Arousal in Male Social Drinkers." Behavior Research and Therapy 21,4:365-373. [5.1]

Barnett, Nona J. and Hubert S. Feild
1977 "Sex Differences in University Students' Attitudes Toward Rape." Journal of College Student Personnel 18:93-96. [7.1]

Bechhofer, Laurie and Andrea Parrot
1991 "What is Acquaintance Rape?" Pp. 9-25 in Acquaintance Rape: The Hidden Crime, edited by Andrea Parrot and Laurie Bechhofer. New York: John Wiley and Sons. [6.1]

Belknap, Joanne
1989 "The Sexual Victimization of Unmarried Women by Nonrelative Acquaintances." Pp. 205-218 in Violence in Dating Relationships, edited by Maureen Pirog-Good and Jan Stets. New York: Praeger. [2.4]

Beneke, Timothy
1982 Men on Rape: What They Have to Say About Sexual Violence.. New York: St. Martin's Press. [5.2]

Berger, Ronald; Patricia Searles; Richard Salem; and Beth Ann Pierce
1986 "Sexual Assault in a College Community." Sociological Focus 19,1:1-26. [2.5]

Bergman, Libby
1992 "Dating Violence among High School Students." Social Work 37,1:21-27. [2.6]

Bessmer, Sue
1976 The Laws of Rape. New York: Praeger. [9.1]

Boeringer, Scot B.; Constance Shehan; and Ronald L. Akers
1991 "Social Contexts and Social Learning in Sexual Coercion and Aggression: Assessing the Contribution of Fraternity Membership." Family Relations 40:58-64. [3.2]

Bohmer, Carol
1991 "Acquaintance Rape and the Law." Pp 317-34 in Acquaintance Rape: The Hidden Crime, edited by Andrea Parrot and Laurie Bechhofer. New York: John Wiley and Sons. [9.2]

Bohmer, Carol and Andrea Parrot
1993 Sexual Assault on Campus: The Problem and the Solution. NY: Lexington Books. [9.3]

Bourque, Linda Brookover
1989 Defining Rape. Durham, NC: Duke University Press. [7.2]

Bridges, Judith S. and Christine A. McGrail
1989 "Attributions of Responsibility for Date and Stranger Rape." Sex Roles 21,3/4:273-286. [8.3]

Briere, John and Neil Malamuth
1983 "Self-reported Likelihood of Sexually Aggressive Behavior: Attitudinal versus Sexual Explanations." Journal of Research in Personality 17:315-323. [5.3]

Briere, John; Neil Malamuth; and James V.P. Check
1985 "Sexuality and Rape-Supportive Beliefs." International Journal of Women Studies 8,4:398-403. [7.3]

Brownmiller, Susan
1975 Against Our Will: Men, Women, and Rape. New York: Simon and Schuster. [6.2]

Burgess, Ann Wolbert
1985 "Sexual Victimization of Adolescents." Pp. 123-38 in Rape and Sexual Assault: A Research Handbook, edited by Ann Wolbert Burgess. New York: Garland. [13.1]

Burgess, Ann Wolbert and Lynda Lytle Holmstrom
1974 Rape: Victims of Crisis. Bowie, MD: Robert J. Brady. [13.2]

Burke, Peter; Jan Stets; and Maureen Pirog-Good
1988 "Gender Identity, Self-Esteem and Physical and Sexual Abuse in Dating Relationships." Social Psychology Quarterly 51:272-285. [3.3]

Burkhart, Barry R.
1991 "Conceptual and Practical Analysis of Therapy for Acquaintance Rape Victims." Pp. 287-303 in Acquaintance Rape: The Hidden Crime, edited by Andrea Parrot and Laurie Bechhofer. New York: John Wiley and Sons. [13.3]

Burkhart, Barry R. and Annette L. Stanton
1988 "Sexual Aggression in Acquaintance Relationships." Pp. 43-45 in Violence in Intimate Relationships, edited by G.W. Russell. NY: PMA Publishing Corp. [2.7]

Burt, Martha
1980 "Cultural Myths and Support for Rape." Journal of Personality and Social Behavior 38,2:217-230. [7.4]

Burt, Martha

1991 "Rape Myths and Acquaintance Rape." Pp. 26-40 in Acquaintance Rape: The Hidden Crime, edited by Andrea Parrot and Laurie Bechhofer. New York: John Wiley and Sons. [7.5]

Burt, Martha and R.S. Albin

1981 "Rape Myths, Rape Definitions, and Probability of Conviction." Journal of Applied Social Psychology 11,3:212-230. [7.6]

Burt, Martha and Rhoda E. Estep

1981 "Who is a Victim? Definitional Problems in Sexual Victimization." Victimology 6:15-28. [6.3]

Calhoun, Karen S. and Ruth M. Townsley

1991 "Attributions of Responsibility for Acquaintance Rape." Pp. 57-70 in Acquaintance Rape: The Hidden Crime, edited by Andrea Parrot and Laurie Bechhofer. New York: John Wiley and Sons. [8.4]

Chancer, Lynn S.

1987 "New Bedford, Massachusetts, March 6, 1983-March 22, 1984: The Before and After of a Group Rape." Gender & Society 1:239-260. [12.1]

Check, James V.P. and Neil M. Malamuth

1983 "Sex Role Stereotyping and Reactions to Depictions of Stranger Versus Acquaintance Rape." Journal of Personality and Social Psychology 45,2:344-356. [7.7]

Check, James V.P. and Neil M. Malamuth

1985 "An Empirical Assessment of Some Feminist Hypotheses About Rape." International Journal of Women's Studies 8,4:414-423. [6.4]

Clark, Lorenne M.G. and Debra J. Lewis
1977 Rape: The Price of Coercive Sexuality. Toronto: The Women's Press. [7.8]

Coller, Sarah A. and Patricia A. Resick
1987 "Women's Attributions of Responsibility for Date Rape: The Influence of Empathy and Sex-Role Stereotyping." Violence and Victims 2,2:115-125. [8.5]

Dean, Charles W. and Mary deBruyn-Kops
1982 The Crime and the Consequences of Rape. Springfield, IL: Charles C. Thomas. [2.8]

DeKeseredy, Walter S.
1988 "Woman Abuse in Dating Relationships: The Relevance of Social Support Theory." Journal of Family Violence 3,1:1-13. [6.5]

Dull, Thomas R. and David J. Giacopassi
1987 "Demographic Correlates of Sexual and Dating Attitudes: A Study of Date Rape." Criminal Justice and Behavior 14,2:175-193. [7.9]

Ellis, Lee
1991 "The Drive to Possess and Control as a Motivation for Sexual Behavior: Applications to the Study of Rape." Social Science Information 30,4:663-675. [6.6]

Enke, Janet L. and Lori K. Sudduth
1991 "Educational Reforms." Pp. 149-60 in Sexual Coercion: A Sourcebook on Its Nature, Causes, and Prevention, edited by Elizabeth Grauerholz and Mary A. Koraleowski. Lexington, MA: Lexington Books. [14.2]

Estrich, Susan
1987 Real Rape: How the Legal System Victimizes Women Who Say No. Cambridge: Harvard University Press. [9.4]

Feild, Hubert S. and Leigh R. Bienin
1980 Jurors and Rape: A Study in Psychology and Law. Lexington, MA: Lexington. [9.5]

Feltey, Kathryn M.; Julie J. Ainslie; and Aleta Geib
1991 "Sexual Coercion Attitudes among High School Students: The Influence of Gender and Rape Education." Youth and Society 23,2:229-250. [7.10]

Fenstermaker, Sarah
1989 "Acquaintance Rape on Campus: Attributions of Responsibility and Crime." Pp. 257-271 in Violence in Dating Relationships, edited by Maureen Pirog-Good and Jan Stets. New York: Praeger. [8.6]

Ferguson, Patricia A.; Dolores A. Duthie; and Richard G. Graf
1987 "Attribution of Responsibility to Rapist and Victim: The Influence of Victim's Attractiveness and Rape-Related Information." Journal of Interpersonal Violence 2,3:243-250. [8.7]

Finkelhor, David and Kersti Yllo
1985 License to Rape: Sexual Abuse of Wives. New York: Holt, Rinehart, and Winston. [11.1]

Fischer, Gloria J.
1986 "College Student Attitudes Toward Forcible Date Rape: I. Cognitive Predictors." Archives of Sexual Behavior 15,6:457-466. [7.11]

Fischer, Gloria J.
1986 "College Student Attitudes Toward Forcible Date Rape: Changes after Taking a Human Sexuality Course." Journal of Sex Education and Therapy 12:42-46. [7.12]

Fischer, Gloria J.
1987 "Hispanic and Majority Student Attitudes toward Forcible Date Rape as a Function of Differences in Attitudes toward Women" Sex Roles 17(1/2):93-101. [7.13]

Frieze, Irene
1983 "Investigating the Causes and Consequences of Marital Rape." Signs: Journal of Women in Culture and Society 8:532-553. [11.2]

Garrett-Gooding, Joy and Richard Senter, Jr.
1987 "Attitudes and Acts of Sexual Aggression on a University Campus." Sociological Inquiry 57:348-371. [7.14]

Geis, Gilbert
1971 "Group Sexual Assaults." Medical Aspects of Human Sexuality 5:101-113. [12.2]

Giacopassi, David and R. Thomas Dull
1986 "Gender and Racial Differences in the Acceptance of Rape Myths Within a College Population." Sex Roles 15,1/2:63-75. [7.15]

Gidycz, Christine A. and Mary P. Koss
1991 "The Effects of Acquaintance Rape on the Female Victim." Pp.270-84 in Acquaintance Rape: The Hidden Crime, edited by Andrea Parrot and Laurie Bechhofer. New York: John Wiley and Sons. [13.4]

Gilmartin-Zena, Pat
1988 "Gender Differences in Students' Attitudes Toward Rape." Sociological Focus 21:279-292. [7.16]

Goodchilds, J.D. and G.L. Zellman
1984 "Sexual Signaling and Sexual Aggression in Adolescent Relationships." In Pp. 233-243 in Pornography and Sexual Aggression, edited by N.M. Malamuth and E. Donnerstein. Orlando, FL: Academic Press. [7.17]

Goodchilds, J.D.; G. Zellman; P.B. Johnson; and R. Giarusso
1988 "Adolescents and Their Perceptions of Sexual Interaction Outcomes." Pp. 245-270 in Sexual Assault, Volume II, edited by A.W. Burgess. New York: Garland. [8.8]

Gordon, Margaret T. and Stephanie Riger
1989 The Female Fear: The Social Cost of Rape. Chicago: University of Illinois Press. [7.18]

Greendlinger, Virginia and Donn Byrne
1987 "Coercive Sexual Fantasies of College Men as Predictors of Self-Reported Likelihood to Rape and Overt Sexual Aggression." Journal of Sex Research 23,1:1-11. [5.4]

Gwartney-Gibbs, Patricia A.; Jean Stockard; and Susanne Bohmer
1987 "Learning Courtship Aggression: The Influence of Parents, Peers, and Personal Experiences." Family Relations 36:276-82. [2.9]

Gwartney-Gibbs, Patricia and Jean Stockard
1989 "Courtship Aggression and Mixed-Sex Peer Groups." Pp. 185-204 in Violence in Dating Relationships, edited by Maureen Pirog-Good and Jan Stets. New York: Praeger. [3.4]

Harney, Patricia A. and Charlene L. Muehlenhard
1991 "Factors that Increase the Likelihood of Victimization." Pp.159-75 in Acquaintance Rape: The Hidden Crime, edited by Andrea Parrot and Laurie Bechhofer. New York: John Wiley and Sons. [3.5]

Harney, Patricia A. and Charlene L. Muehlenhard
1991 "Rape." Pp. 3-15 in Sexual Coercion: A Sourcebook on its Nature, Causes, and Prevention, edited by Elizabeth Grauerholz and Mary A. Koraleowski. Lexington, MA: Lexington Books. [2.10]

Heilbrun, Alfred B. and Maura P. Loftus
1986 "The Role of Sadism and Peer Pressure in the Sexual Aggression of Male College Students." Journal of Sex Research 22,3:320-332. [5.5]

Jacobson, Marsha B. and Paula M. Popovich
1983 "Victim Attractiveness and Perceptions of Responsibility in an Ambiguous Rape Case." Psychology of Women Quarterly 8,1:100-104. [8.9]

Jenkins, Megan and Faye Dambrot
1987 "The Attribution of Date Rape: Observer's Attitudes and Sexual Experiences and The Dating Situation." Journal of Applied Social Psychology 17,10:875-895. [8.10]

Johnson, G. David; Gloria J. Palileo; and Norma B. Gray
1991 "'Date Rape' on a Southern Campus: Reports from 1991." Sociology and Social Research 76,2:37-44. [2.11]

Johnson, James D. and Lee A. Jackson, Jr.
1988 "Assessing the Effects of Factors that Might Underlie the Differential Perception of Acquaintance and Stranger Rape." Sex Roles 19,1/2:37-45. [7.19]

Johnson, James D. and Inger Russ
1989 "Effects of Salience of Consciousness-Raising Information on Perceptions of Acquaintance Versus Stranger Rape." Journal of Applied Psychology 19:1182-1197. [7.20]

Kanin, Eugene J.
1957 "Male Aggression in Dating-Courtship Relations." American Journal of Sociology 63:197-204. [2.12]

Kanin, Eugene J.
1965 "Male Sex Aggression and Three Psychiatric Hypotheses." Journal of Sex Research 1:221-231. [5.6]

Kanin, Eugene J.
1967 "An Examination of Sexual Aggression as a Response to Sexual Frustration." Journal of Marriage and the Family 29:428-433. [5.7]

Kanin, Eugene J.
1967 "Reference Groups and Sex Conduct Norm Violations." Sociological Quarterly 8:495-504. [5.8]

Kanin, Eugene J.
1969 "Selected Dyadic Aspects of Male Sex Aggression." Journal of Sex Research 5:12-28. [2.13]

Kanin, Eugene J.
1971 "Sexually Aggressive College Males." The Journal of College Student Personnel 12:107-110. [5.9]

Kanin, Eugene J.
1984 "Date Rape: Unofficial Criminals and Victims." Victimology 9,1:95-108. [5.10]

Kanin, Eugene J.
1985 "Date Rapists: Differential Sexual Socialization and Relative Deprivation." Archives of Sexual Behavior 14,3:219-231. [5.11]

Kanin, Eugene J.; Eugene C. Jackson; and Edward M. Levine
1987 "Personal Sexual History and Punitive Judgements for Rape." Psychological Reports 61:439-442. [7.21]

Kanin, Eugene and Stanley R. Parcell
1977 "Sexual Aggression: A Second Look at the Offended Female." Archives of Sexual Behavior 6,1:67-76. [2.14]

Koss, Mary P.; Christine A. Gidycz; and Nadine Wisniewski
1987 "The Scope of Rape: Incidence and Prevalence of Sexual Aggression and Victimization in a National Sample of Higher Education Students." Journal of Consulting and Clinical Psychology 55,2:162-170. [2.22]

Koss, Mary P. and Mary R. Harvey
1991 The Rape Victim: Clinical and Community Interventions. Newbury Park: Sage. [13.8]

Koss, Mary; Kenneth Leonard; Dana Beezley; and Cheryl Oros
1985 "Nonstranger Sexual Aggression: A Discriminant Analysis of the Psychological Characteristics of Undetected Offenders." Sex Roles 12,9/10:981-993. [5.13]

Koss, Mary P. and Cheryl J. Oros
1982 "Sexual Experiences Survey: A Research Instrument Investigating Sexual Aggression and Victimization." Journal of Consulting and Clinical Psychology 50,3:455-457. [2.23]

Lafree, Gary
1989 Rape and Criminal Justice: The Social Construction of Sexual Assault. Belmont, CA: Wadsworth. [9.6]

Lane, Katherine E. and Patricia Gwartney-Gibbs
1985 "Violence in the Context of Dating and Sex." Journal of Family Issues 6,1:45-69. [2.24]

LaPlante, Marcia; Naomi McCormick; and Gary Brannigan
1980 "Living the Sexual Script: College Student's Views of Influence in Sexual Encounters." Journal of Sex Research 16,4:338-355. [4.6]

L'Armand, K. and A. Pepitone
1982 "Judgments of Rape: A Study of Victim-Rapist Relationship and Victim Sexual History." Personality and Social Psychology Bulletin 8,1:134-139. [7.22]

Levine, Edward M. and Eugene J. Kanin
1987 "Sexual Violence Among Dates and Acquaintances: Trends and Their Implications for Marriage and Family." Journal of Family Violence 2,1:55-65. [3.7]

Levine-MacCombie, Joyce and Mary P. Koss
1986 "Acquaintance Rape: Effective Avoidance Strategies." Psychology of Women Quarterly 10:311-320. [14.3]

Lewin, Miriam
1985 "Unwanted Intercourse: The Difficulty of Saying No." Psychology of Women Quarterly 9:184-192. [7.23]

Lott, Bernice; Mary Ellen Reilly; and Dale R. Howard
1982 "Sexual Assault and Harassment: A Campus Community Case Study." Signs: Journal of Women in Culture and Society 8,2:296-319. [10.1]

Lundberg-Love, Paula and Robert Geffner
1989 "Date Rape: Prevalence, Risk Factors, and a Proposed Model." Pp. 169-184 in Violence in Dating Relationships, edited by Maureen Pirog-Good and Jan Stets. New York: Praeger. [2.25]

Lyons, Arthur W. and Joanne Regina
1986 "Mock Jurors' Behavior as a Function of Sex and Exposure to an Educational Videotape about Jury Duty." Psychological Reports 58:599-604. [9.7]

Madigan, Lee and Nancy C. Gamble
1991 The Second Rape: Society's Continued Betrayal of the Victim. New York: Lexington Books. [13.9]

Mahoney, E.R.; Michael D. Shively; and Marsha Traw
1986 "Sexual Coercion and Assault: Male Socialization and Female Risk." Sexual Coercion & Assault 1,1:2-8. [5.14]

Makepeace, James
1986 "Gender Differences in Courtship Violence Victimization." Family Relations 35:383-388. [3.8]

Malamuth, Neil M.
1981 "Rape Proclivity Among Males." Journal of Social Issues 37,4:138-157. [5.15]

Malamuth, Neil M.
1986 "Predictors of Naturalistic Sexual Aggression." Journal of Personality and Social Psychology 50:953-962. [5.16]

Malamuth, Neil M. and James Check
1980 "Sexual Arousal to Rape and Consenting Depictions: The Importance of the Woman's Arousal." Journal of Abnormal Psychology 89,6:763-766. [7.24]

Malamuth, Neil M. and Karol E. Dean
1991 "Attraction to Sexual Aggression." Pp. 229-48 in Acquaintance Rape: The Hidden Crime, edited by Andrea Parrot and Laurie Bechhofer. New York: John Wiley and Sons. [5.17]

Malamuth, Neil M.; Scott Haber; and Seymour Feshbach
1980 "Testing Hypotheses Regarding Rape: Exposure to Sexual Violence, Sex Differences, and the 'Normality' of Rapists." Journal of Research in Personality 14:121-137. [7.25]

Malamuth, Neil M.; Maggie Heim; and Seymour Feshbach
1980 "Sexual Responsiveness of College Students to Rape Depictions: Inhibitory and Disinhibitory Effects." Journal of Personality and Social Psychology 38, 3:399-408. [7.26]

Mandoki, Catalina A. and Barry R. Burkhart
1991 "Women as Victims: Antecedents and Consequences of Acquaintance Rape" Pp.176-91 in Acquaintance Rape: The Hidden Crime, edited by Andrea Parrot and Laurie Bechhofer. New York: John Wiley and Sons. [3.9]

Mann, Cythnia A.; Michael L. Hecht; and Kristin B. Valentine
1988 "Performance in a Social Context: Date Rape versus Date Right." Central States Speech Journal 39,3/4:269-280. [14.4]

Margolin, Leslie; Melody Miller; and Patricia Moran
1989 "When a Kiss is Not Just a Kiss: Relating Violations of Consent in Kissing to Rape Myth Acceptance." Sex Roles 20:231-243. [7.27]

Martin, Patricia Yancey and Robert A. Hummer
1989 "Fraternities and Rape on Campus." Gender & Society 3,4:457-473. [10.2]

McCahill, T.W.; Linda Meyer; and A. Fischman
1979 The Aftermath of Rape. Lexington: Lexington Books. [3.10]

McCormick, Naomi B.
1979 "Come-ons and Put-offs: Unmarried Students' Strategies for Having and Avoiding Sexual Intercourse." Psychology of Women Quarterly 4,2:194-211. [14.5]

McKinney, Kathleen
1986 "Measures of Verbal, Physical, and Sexual Dating Violence by Gender." Free Inquiry in Creative Sociology 14,1:55-60. [3.11]

McKinney, Kathleen
1986 "Perceptions of Courtship Violence: Gender Difference and Involvement." Free Inquiry in Creative Sociology 14,1:61-66. [7.28]

Miller, Beverly and Jon C. Marshall
1987 "Coercive Sex on the University Campus." Journal of College Student Personnel 28:38-47. [2.26]

Mills, Crystal S. and Barbara J. Granoff
1992 "Date and Acquaintance Rape Among a Sample of College Students." Social Work 37,6:504-509. [2.27]

Muehlenhard, Charlene L.
1988 "Misinterpreted Dating Behaviors and the Risk of Date Rape." Journal of Social and Clinical Psychology 6,1:20-37. [7.29]

Muehlenhard, Charlene L. and Polly L. Falcon
1990 "Men's Heterosocial Skill and Attitudes Toward Women as Predictors of Verbal Sexual Coercion and Forceful Rape." Sex Roles 23,5/6:241-259. [2.28]

Muehlenhard, Charlene L.; Debra E. Friedman; and Celeste M. Thomas
1985 "Is Date Rape Justifiable?: The Effects of Dating Activity, Who Initiated, Who Paid, and Men's Attitudes Toward Women." Psychology of Women Quarterly 9:297-310. [7.30]

Muehlenhard, Charlene and Lisa C. Hollabaugh
1988 "Do Women Sometimes Say No When They Mean Yes? The Prevalence and Correlates of Women's Token Resistance to Sex." Journal of Personality and Social Psychology 54,5:872-879. [14.6]

Muehlenhard, Charlene L. and Melaney A. Linton
1987 "Date Rape and Sexual Aggression in Dating Situations: Incidence and Risk Factors." Journal of Counseling Psychology 34,2:186-196. [3.12]

Muehlenhard, Charlene L. and Jennifer L. Schrag
1991 "Nonviolent Sexual Coercion." Pp. 115-28 in Acquaintance Rape: The Hidden Crime, edited by Andrea Parrot and Laurie Bechhofer. New York: John Wiley and Sons. [6.7]

Murnen, Sarah K.; Annette Perot; and Donn Byrne
1989 "Coping with Unwanted Sexual Activity: Normative Responses, Situational Determinants, and Individual Differences." Journal of Sex Research 26,1:85-106. [2.29]

O'Sullivan, Chris S.
1991 "Gang Rape on Campus." Pp. 140-56 in Acquaintance Rape: The Hidden Crime, edited by Andrea Parrot and Laurie Bechhofer. New York: John Wiley and Sons. [12.3]

Parrot, Andrea
1989 "Acquaintance Rape among Adolescents: Identifying Risk Groups and Intervention Strategies." Journal of Social Work and Human Sexuality 8,1:47-61. [13.10]

Parrot, Andrea
1991 "Institutional Response: How can Acquaintance Rape be Prevented." Pp 355-67 in Acquaintance Rape: The Hidden Crime, edited by Andrea Parrot and Laurie Bechhofer. New York: John Wiley and Sons. [14.7]

Parrot, Andrea
1991 "Medical Community Response to Acquaintance Rape Recommendations." Pp 304-16 in Acquaintance Rape: The Hidden Crime, edited by Andrea Parrot and Laurie Bechhofer. New York: John Wiley and Sons. [13.11]

Parrot Andrea
1991 "Recommendations for College Policies and Procedures to Deal with Acquaintance Rape." Pp. 368-80 in Acquaintance Rape: The Hidden Crime, edited by Andrea Parrot and Laurie Bechhofer. New York: John Wiley and Sons. [14.8]

Parrot, Andrea and Laurie Bechhofer
1991 Acquaintance Rape: The Hidden Crime. NY: John Wiley. [2.30]

Peterson, Steven and Bettina Franzese
1987 "Correlates of College Men's Sexual Abuse of Women." Journal of College Student Personnel May:223-228. [5.18]

Pineau, Lois
1989 "Date Rape: A Feminist Analysis." Law and Philosophy 8,2:217-243. [6.8]

Ploughman, Penelope and John Stensrud
1986 "The Ecology of Rape Victimization: A Case Study of Buffalo, New York." Genetic, Social, and General Psychology Monographs 112,3:303-324. [3.13]

Rapaport, Karen and Barry R. Burkhart
1984 "Personality and Attitudinal Characteristics of Sexually Coercive College Males." Journal of Abnormal Psychology 93,2:216-221. [5.19]

Rapaport, Karen R. and C. Dale Posey
1991 "Sexually Coercive College Males." Pp 217-28 in Acquaintance Rape: The Hidden Crime, edited by Andrea Parrot and Laurie Bechhofer. New York: John Wiley and Sons. [5.20]

Richardson, Deborah and Jennifer L. Campbell
1982 "Alcohol and Rape: The Effect of Alcohol on Attributions of Blame for Rape." Personality and Social Psychology Bulletin 8,3:468-476. [8.11]

Richardson, Deborah R. and Georgina S. Hammock
1991 "Alcohol and Acquaintance Rape." Pp. 83-95 in Acquaintance Rape: The Hidden Crime, edited by Andrea Parrot and Laurie Bechhofer. New York: John Wiley and Sons. [3.14]

Rivera, George and Robert Regoli
1987 "Sexual Victimization Experiences of Sorority Women." Sociology and Social Research 72:39-42. [2.31]

Rouse, Linda; Richard Breen; and Marilyn Howell
1988 "Abuse in Intimate Relationships: A Comparison of Married and Dating College Students." Journal of Interpersonal Violence 3,4:414-429. [3.15]

Rowan, Edward L. and Judith B. Rowen
1984 "Rape and the College Student: Multiple Crisis in Late Adolescence." Pp. 234-250 in Victims of Sexual Aggression: Treatment of Children, Women, and Men, edited by Irving P. Stuart and Joanne G. Greer. New York: VanNostrand Reinhold. [13.12]

Rozee, Patricia D.; Py Bateman; and Theresa Gilmore
1991 "The Personal Perspective of Acquaintance Rape Prevention: The Three-Tier Approach." Pp 337-354 in Acquaintance Rape: The Hidden Crime, edited by Andrea Parrot and Laurie Bechhofer. New York: John Wiley and Sons. [14.9]

Russell, Diana E.H.
1975 The Politics of Rape: The Victim's Perspective. New York: Stein and Day. [3.16]

Russell, Diana E.H.
1984 Sexual Exploitation: Rape, Child Sexual Abuse, and Workplace Harassment. Beverly Hills: Sage. [2.32]

Russell, Diana E.H.
1990 Rape in Marriage, Second Edition. Indianapolis: Indiana University Press. [11.3]

Russell, Diana E.H.
1991 "Wife Rape." Pp. 129-39 in Acquaintance Rape: The Hidden Crime. New York: John Wiley and Sons. [11.4]

Sanday, Peggy Reeves
1990 Fraternity Gang Rape: Sex, Brotherhood, and Privilege on Campus. New York: New York University Press. [12.4]

Sandberg, Genell; Thomas Jackson; and Patricia Petretic-Jackson
1987 "College Students' Attitudes Regarding Sexual Coercion and Aggression: Developing Educational and Preventive Strategies." Journal of College Student Personnel 28:302-311. [7.31]

Sanders, William B.
1980 Rape and Women's Identity. Beverly Hills: Sage. [6.9]

Sarrel, Philip M. and William H. Masters
1982 "Sexual Molestation of Men by Women." Archives of Sexual Behavior 11,2:117-131. [3.17]

Schneider, D. Jean; Donald Blydenburgh; and Gail Craft
1981 "Some Factors For Analysis in Sexual Assault." Social Science and Medicine 15A:55-61. [3.18]

Schultz, LeRoy G. and Jan DeSavage
1975 "Rape and Rape Attitudes on a College Campus." Pp. 77-88 in Rape Victimology, edited by LeRoy Schultz. Springfield, IL: Charles C. Thomas. [7.32]

Schwartz, Martin D.
1991 "Humanist Sociology and Date Rape on the College Campus." Humanity and Society 15,3:304-316. [10.3]

Schwendinger, Julia R. and Herman Schwendinger
1983 Rape and Inequality. Beverly Hills: Sage. [6.10]

Shotland, Lance R.
1985 "A Preliminary Model of Some Causes of Date Rape." Academic Psychology Bulletin 7:187-200. [6.11]

Shotland, Lance R.
1989 "A Model of the Causes of Date Rape in Developing and Close Relationships." Pp. 247-270 in Close Relationships, edited by C. Hendrick. Newbury Park, CA: Sage. [6.12]

Shotland, Lance R.
1992 "A Theory of the Causes of Courtship Rape: Part 2." Journal of Social Issues 48,1:127-148. [6.13]

Shotland, Lance R. and Jane M. Craig
1988 "Can Men and Women Differentiate Between Friendly and Sexually Interested Behavior?" Social Psychology Quarterly 51:66-73. [4.7]

Shotland, Lance R. and Lynne Goodstein
1983 "Just Because She Doesn't Want to Doesn't Mean It's Rape: An Experimentally Based Causal Model of the Perception of Rape in a Dating Situation." Social Psychology Quarterly 46,3:220-232. [8.12]

Shotland, Lance R. and Lynne Goodstein
1992 "Sexual Precedence Reduces the Perceived Legitimacy of Sexual Refusal: An Examination of Attributions Concerning Date Rape and Consensual Sex." Journal of Personality and Social Psychology 18:756-764. [7.33]

Sigal, Janet; Margaret Gibbs; Bonnie Adams; and Richard Derfler
1988 "The Effect of Romantic and Nonromantic Films on Perception of Female Friendly and Seductive Behavior." Sex Roles 19,9/10:545-554. [4.8]

Sorenson, Susan B.; Judith A. Stein; Judith M. Siegel; Jacqueline M. Golding; and M. Audrey Burnham
1987 "The Prevalence of Adult Sexual Assault: The Los Angeles Epidemiologic Catchment Area Project." American Journal of Epidemiology 126,6:1154-1164. [2.33]

Spohn, Cassia and Julie Horney
1992 Rape Law Reform: A Grass Roots Revolution and Its Impact. New York: Plenum Press. [9.8]

Stanko, Elizabeth Anne
1987 "Ordinary Fear: Women, Violence, and Personal Safety." Pp. 155-164 in Violence Against Women: The Bloody Footprints, edited by Pauline Bart and Eileen Geil Moran. Newbury Park: Sage. [7.34]

Stets, Jan E. and Maureen A. Pirog-Good
1989 "Patterns of Physical and Sexual Abuse for Men and Women in Dating Relationships: A Descriptive Analysis." Journal of Family Violence 4,1:63-76. [2.34]

Struckman-Johnson, Cindy
1991 "Male Victims of Acquaintance Rape." Pp 192-214 in Acquaintance Rape: The Hidden Crime, edited by Andrea Parrot and Laurie Bechhofer. New York: John Wiley and Sons. [3.19]

Temkin, Jennifer
1986 "Women, Rape and Law Reform." Pp. 16-39 in Rape, edited by Sylvana Tomaselli and Roy Porter. Oxford: Basil Blackwell. [9.9]

Tetreault, Patricia A. and Mark A. Barnett
1987 "Reactions to Stranger and Acquaintance Rape." Psychology of Women Quarterly 11:353-358. [8.13]

Tieger, Todd
1981 "Self-rated Likelihood of Raping and the Social Perception of Rape." Journal of Research in Personality 15:147-158. [8.14]

Ward, Sally; Kathy Chapman; Ellen Cohn; Susan White; and Kirk Williams
1991 "Acquaintance Rape and the College Social Scene." Family Relations 40:65-71. [2.35]

Warshaw, Robin
1988 I Never Called It Rape: The Ms. Report on Recognizing, Fighting and Surviving Date and Acquaintance Rape. New York: Harper and Row. [2.36]

Warshaw, Robin and Andrea Parrot
1991 "The Contribution of Sex-Role Socialization to Acquaintance Rape." Pp. 73-82 in Acquaintance Rape: The Hidden Crime, edited by Andrea Parrot and Laurie Bechhofer. New York: John Wiley and Sons. [4.9]

White, Jacquelyn W. and John A. Humphrey
1991 "Young People's Attitudes Toward Acquaintance Rape."

Pp. 43-56 in Acquaintance Rape: The Hidden Crime, edited by Andrea Parrot and Laurie Bechhofer. New York: John Wiley and Sons. [7.35]

Wilson, Kenneth; Rebecca Faison and; G.M. Britton
1983 "Cultural Aspects of Male Sex Aggression." Deviant Behavior 4:241-255. [5.21]

Wilson, Wayne and Robert Durrenberger
1982 "Comparisons of Rape and Attempted Rape Victims." Psychological Reports 50:198. [14.10]

Wyer, Robert S.; Galen V. Bordenhausen; and Theresa F. Gorman.
1985 "Cognitive Mediators of Reactions to Rape." Journal of Personality and Social Psychology 48,2:324-338. [7.36]

Yllo, Kersti and David Finkelhor
1985 "Marital Rape." Pp. 146-155 in Rape and Sexual Assault: A Research Handbook, edited by Ann Wolbert Burgess. New York: Garland. [11.5]

Youn, Gahyun
1987 "On Using Public Media for Prevention of Rape." Psychological Reports 61:237-238. [14.11]

2

INCIDENCE OF ACQUAINTANCE RAPE

2.1 Ageton, Suzanne S.
1983 Sexual Assault among Adolescents. Lexington, MA: Lexington Books.

Purpose: The purpose of this research was to describe the extent and nature of rapes committed by and against adolescents.
Method: A survey was conducted with a nationally-representative panel of 1,725 youths age 11-17 in 1976, and this panel was followed up for five consecutive years (1977-1981). The questionnaire included items regarding both commission of rape and rape victimization experiences.
Findings: Regarding female subjects, rapes and attempted rapes were reported by an annual average of about 7% of the female sample. This rate is generally higher than that presented in other, "official" sources of crime reports, indicating the utility of private, age-appropriate interview techniques in obtaining information about victimization from youths. Older girls and those in urban areas appear to have experienced greater risk for rape during the survey period. No race or social class differences in risk for rape victimization were noted. Assaults of younger teens were more likely to involve known offenders (over 90% of cases), but the proportion of stranger offenders increased with the age of victims. Assaults were about equally likely to take place in a vehicle, the victim's home, and the offender's home. Verbal coercion was the most frequently-reported type of force used. A number of factors

were found to be associated with vulnerability to sexual assault, including family climate, peer relationships, school integration, delinquent behavior, and the experience of other forms of victimization. Information on reporting, and on both short- and long-term effects of sexual assault for victims, is also provided.

Regarding male subjects, commission of rape and attempted rape was reported by an annual average of about 3% of the male sample. The likelihood of raping increased with age. A working-class background was associated with a decreased likelihood of raping compared to the lower and middle classes, while residence in suburban or rural areas (compared to urban) was associated with the commission of multiple rape offenses. No racial differences in rape offending were observed. The most common assault location reported by perpetrators was the victim's home. Assaults committed in vehicles declined with the age of the offender, while those committed outside increased. Verbal coercion was the most frequently-reported type of force used. Family climate, peer relationships, school integration/success, and delinquent behavior were found to be associated with the likelihood of committing rape/attempted rape.

2.2 Aizenman, Marta and Georgette Kelley
1988 "The Incidence of Violence and Acquaintance Rape in Dating Relationships Among College Men and Women." Journal of College Student Development 29:305-311.

Purpose: To examine the incidence of violence and acquaintance rape, the circumstances under which it occurs, attitudes toward violence in a romantic relationship, the relationship between abuse suffered and abuse given, and the relationship of abuse to personality variables.
Method: Of the 400 men and 400 women who received the survey, 51% of the women and 35% of the men completed and returned it. All were undergraduates. Respondents were asked whether they had been abused as children, type of abuse, and whether it was casual or steady. Other items addressed attitudes

toward violence in relationships. They were also asked about experiences of date rape and forced sexual encounters. Finally, they were asked to rate their feelings of well-being, self-confidence, and other psychological variables.
Findings: A higher percentage of women than men reported being abused. There was no significant gender-based difference in those who had perpetrated abuse. Most cases of abuse within a relationship happened in an ongoing, steady one. For both sexes, being abused related to lack of sense of control over their own behavior and perpetrating abuse. 95% of the students objected to the use of violence. A significant difference was found between men (7%) and women (1%) who thought violence could be helpful in a relationship. Over half of each sample indicated that they knew someone who was involved in a violent relationship. More women than men reported being fondled or sexually touched as children, and this was strongly related to later experiences with forced sexual contact. A lack of a sense of well-being was strongly related to having been inappropriately fondled as a child, among women. Concerning punishment as a child, women were punished more than men, and this punishment was related to feelings of well-being and being abused in a later relationship. For men, punishment was related to considering the punishment abusive and not being comfortable with their sexuality.

2.3 Amick, Angelynne E. and Karen S. Calhoun
1987 "Resistance to Sexual Aggression: Personality, Attitudinal, and Situational Factors." Archives of Sexual Behavior 16,2:153-162.

Purpose: Resistance to sexual aggression is assessed and tested against three theoretical models that predict resistance to acquaintance rape.
Method: Female undergraduate students responded to the Sexual Experiences Survey (Koss and Oros 1982) and a series of questions that measured victim precipitation, social control, and situational blame.
Findings: Three-fourths of the participants reported sexual

victimization, the majority which, 94%, involved acquaintances. Sixty-nine percent indicated that their nonconsent was very clear with 58% resisting with physical force and 42% with verbal pleas. The women who successfully resisted sexual assaults were found to possess significantly more initiative , persistence, and leadership than those who were unsuccessful. The situational blame model provided the most productive variables for predicting resistance. Specifically, previous intimacy with the offender affected the victim's likelihood of resisting. Unsuccessful resisters were more likely to be involved in a more steady dating relationship and had a higher frequency and intensity of sexual intimacy with the offender than resisters.

2.4 Belknap, Joanne
1989 "The Sexual Victimization of Unmarried Women by Nonrelative Acquaintances." Pp. 205-18 in Violence in Dating Relationships, edited by Maureen Pirog-Good and Jan Stets. New York: Praeger.

Purpose: To extend research on date rape beyond college students and analyze descriptions of victims, offenders, the offense, victims' responses, and degree of injury of unmarried women.
Method: Uses a sample of 212 unmarried women, 12 years of age and older, from the National Crime Survey data between 1973 and 1982. Reports and compares victim and offense characteristics in acquaintance, well-known, and all nonrelative rapes.
Findings: Characteristics of Victim: Approximately 80% of nonrelative rape victims were between the ages of 16 and 34 and 90% were from lower economic levels. Characteristics of Offense: Rape attempts by offender who knew the victim well were more likely to result in completed rapes than attempts by acquaintances. Rapes by nonrelatives were least likely to occur in the winter, but most likely to occur between the 6:00 PM and Midnight. 12% of nonrelative rapes involved weapons. 41% of victims reported rapes to the police, Description of Injuries and Self Defense: 75% of nonrelative victims received one or more

injuries during attack. Rape by well-known offenders was more likely to result in injury that rape by an acquaintance. 40% required medical attention. Over half of victims attempted to stop the rape with physical force and 43% with reasoning. Practice and policy implications are provided.

2.5 Berger, Ronald; Patricia Searles; Richard Salem; and Beth Ann Pierce
1986 "Sexual Assault in a College Community." Sociological Focus 19:1-26.

Purpose: To analyze rape and sexual assault within the context of the everyday experiences of men and women; to report on a survey of college women regarding the normative climate in a college community.
Method: A mail questionnaire to a random sample of sophomore, junior, and senior women at an undergraduate institution. Questions were asked about sexual contact involving force or threat of force or lack of consent; attempted sexual assault; and campus and community safety. The response rate was 53.9%. The survey results were supplemented by more in-depth qualitative comments solicited in the questionnaire.
Findings: Twenty-four percent of the women had experienced forced sexual contact; twenty percent had experienced non-forced but unwanted sexual contact; and seven percent had experienced unsuccessful attempts at forced contact. These quantitative results document the pervasiveness of unwanted sexual contact. The qualitative comments by the women indicate that women have been socialized to accept male sexual aggression. The authors conclude that sexual assault is culturally normative in our society.

2.6 Bergman, Libby
1992 "Dating Violence among High School Students." Social Work 37,1:21-27.

Purpose: To estimate the prevalence and characteristics of sexual

and physical dating violence and to analyze relationships between demographic and dating characteristics and dating violence.
Method: A self administered questionnaire was distributed and completed by a sample of 631 students (337 men and 294 women) in three high schools (a rural, suburban, and urban). Data concerning sexual and physical dating violence, dating characteristics, and demographic characteristics was gathered. Dating violence was categorized into physical, sexual, and severe (both physical and sexual). Only information on sexual and severe violence is provided in this abstract.
Findings: 15.7 percent of the women and 4.4 percent of the men reported experiencing sexual dating violence. 24.6 percent of the women and 9.9 percent of the men reported severe violence. After experiencing the violence, the majority of students did not report it to anyone. Over half (54.7%) of the women continued to date their partner after sexual violence. Repeat violence was fairly consistent. Sexual violence was experienced by 41.5 percent of the women on the first date. Results from multiple regression analysis revealed that high numbers of dating partners, frequent dating, and low grade point averages in school are related to severe dating violence. Suburban schools had the statistically significant higher rates of severe dating violence and sexual violence. Implications for practice are provided.

2.7 Burkhart, Barry R. and Annette L. Stanton
1988 "Sexual Aggression in Acquaintance Relationships." Pp. 43-65 in Violence in Intimate Relationships, edited by Gordon W. Russell. New York: PMA Publishing.

Purpose: A comprehensive review of the literature on acquaintance rape. The chapter focuses on incidence, characteristics of participants, and dynamics. Provides an excellent overview of research to date of publication.
Method: Review of literature.
Findings: Research was cited for incidence rates among college women. Consistent result were found to support that the majority

of women experience some type of offensive sexual behavior during dating, and at least 25% report nonconsensual intercourse or attempted rape. Koss (1985) estimated at least 10 times as many rapes occur than are reported officially. Among men, self-reports indicate that about 29% report not using any type of coercion, and 15% admitted having intercourse against the woman's will.

Characteristics of victims and perpetrators were also reviewed. Much of the research concerning women as victims generally reports relations between previous sexual victimization and the level of violence used. Other models including dating frequency, number of partners, self-esteem, and identification with traditional sex-roles have also been associated with victimization. Offender characteristics include belief in traditional sex roles, acceptance of "rape myths," and sexual experience. The overall conclusion drawn is that there is support for a characteristic, as well as social, element of sexual aggression.

The literature on acquaintance rape as a social phenomenon indicates that rape-supportive beliefs stem from a wider net of sex-role socialization and adversarial beliefs concerning them. This attitudinal phenomenon is deeply ingrained in our culture and serves to legitimize coercive sexuality.

2.8 Dean, Charles W. and Mary deBruyn-Kops
1982 The Crime and the Consequences of Rape. Springfield, IL: Charles C. Thomas.

Purpose: The purpose of this review is to present data on the frequency and dynamics of rape, characteristics of victims and offenders, public attitudes about rape, consequences for victims, institutional reactions, and prevention information.
Method: Research Review; Statistics are drawn mainly from studies done in the late 1970's.
Findings: Part I describes the incidence, forms (including rape by acquaintances), and social correlates of rape. Part II reviews legal and medical procedures for investigating rape, consequences for victims, and available support services for victims. Part III

reviews and discusses available evidence on resisting rape and minimizing physical harm during rape.

2.9 Gwartney-Gibbs, Patricia A.; Jean Stockard; and Susanne Bohmer
1987 "Learning Courtship Aggression: The Influence of Parents, Peers, and Personal Experiences." Family Relations 36:276-282.

Purpose: To apply social learning theory to courtship aggression and analyze the influence of parents, peers, and personal experiences on learning aggressive dating behavior.
Method: Mail surveys were sent to a random sample of undergraduate students. Data were collected on experiences of inflicting and sustaining aggressive behavior in dating, and the use of aggression by parents, peers, and dating partners. Although both physical and sexual aggression are included in the analysis, only the results concerning sexual aggression are be discussed in this abstract.
Findings: Results reveal a statistically significant relationship between experience with sexual aggression and violence in dating relationships and infliction of sexual aggression by men. Four aspects of social learning, victimization of female peers, sexually aggressive male peers, no experience with courtship violence and experiencing sexual aggression and violence were significantly related to sustaining sexual aggression by men. For women, having no aggressive male peer or victimized female peers, having victimized female peers only, and no experience with courtship aggression were related to sustaining sexual aggression in dating relationships. Based on their analysis, the authors conclude that the study overall finds support for the theory that individuals learn courtship aggression from aggressive parents, peers, and dating partners.

2.10 Harney, Patricia A. and Charlene L. Muehlenhard
1991 "Rape." Pp. 3-15 in Sexual Coercion: A

Sourcebook on its Nature, Causes, and Prevention, edited by Elizabeth Grauerholz and Mary A. Koraleowski. Lexington, MA: Lexington Books.

Purpose: To review the literature on definitions of rape, incidence and prevalence of rape, characteristics of rapists, and consequences of rape. Only the discussion of acquaintance rape is presented in this abstract.
Method: Integrative review of literature.
Findings: Definitions of rape: Legal definitions of rape are based on issues of force and consent. Generally only aggravated rape involving among other things, no relationship between victim and perpetrator, is viewed in the legal system as "real rape." Force and nonconsent are more easily determined with aggravated or stranger rape cases. However, when rape occurs between acquaintances, interpretation of the law is not as clear. As a result, those involved in the criminal justice system, including police officers, jurors, attorneys, and judges, rarely perceive forced intercourse between acquaintances as rape. Researchers avoid this bias by using the legal definition of rape but avoiding the term "rape." Incidence and prevalence: Studies found that between 15 and 24 percent of women have been raped and that most of these rapes occur between acquaintances. Characteristics of rapists: Conclusions vary based on methodology used in the study, especially sample selection. Many studies are based on samples of incarcerated rapists or police reports which generally exclude acquaintance rapists. Alternative methods have been utilized but most of these have some problems as well. Characteristics of self-reported sexually aggressive men include condonation of rape and violence against women, traditional gender role attitudes, sexual experience, hostility towards women, dominance during sex, sexual arousal by rape depictions, irresponsibility, memberships in peer groups that urge sexual activity. Social control theory accurately explains sexual aggression as a result of a society containing rape supportive beliefs reinforced by power differences between men and women. Consequences of rape: Studies show that survivors of rape

experience high levels of anxiety, depression, psychiatric symptoms, poor social adjustment, and sexual dysfunctions. Three theoretical perspectives have been developed to explain the consequences of rape: crisis theory, social learning theory, and cognitive appraisal theory. While one study found few differences in consequences between acquaintance and stranger rapes, more studies are needed to investigate possible differences.

2.11 Johnson, G. David; Gloria J. Palileo; and Norma B. Gray. 1991 "'Date Rape' on a Southern Campus: Reports From 1991." Sociology and Social Research 76,2:37-44.

Purpose: The study measures the incidence of date rape on the campus of University of South Alabama. It also examines criticisms of the date rape movement by comparing the data from this study to findings reported in the Koss et al (1985) national multi-campus survey.
Method: Undergraduate students, 511 males and 666 females, were chosen to participate in this study. Males and females responded to different surveys. Two versions of each questionnaire, yielding a total of four questionnaires, were randomly distributed to students. The two versions included a full set of sexual victimization/aggression questions developed by Koss and Oros (1982) and the other was a shorter version.
Findings: The data indicate similar overall findings to the Koss study. The Southern sample, however, differed significantly for the following items: a larger percentage of women in the present study indicated that they had given in to sex play because a man used his authority over her; and men were less likely to admit attempted intercourse and actual intercourse with a woman via alcohol and drugs in the current study. However, men in the Southern sample were more likely to admit to forced intercourse than men in the national sample.

Several differences were found between the long and short forms. Men were more likely to admit forced sexual intercourse on the long form and women were more likely to define their experience as rape in the short form. Finally, more than half of the respondents in the present study reported that there were times that they did not clearly communicate their sexual intentions to their partner, often saying "no" when they meant "yes" This finding in particular supports the criticisms of the anti-rape movement.

2.12 Kanin, Eugene J.
1957 "Male Aggression in Dating-Courtship Relations." American Journal of Sociology 63:197-204.

Purpose: The study measures the incidence of male aggression in dating-courtship relationships.
Method: Undergraduate women responded to a questionnaire that asked about their offensive and displeasing sexual experiences, ranging from petting above the waist to sexual intercourse. To be considered offensive and displeasing, the actions had to be "accompanied by menacing threats or coercive infliction of physical pain."
Findings: Thirty four percent of the respondents had experienced attempted intercourse and 14% attempted intercourse with violence. These two experiences were more likely to occur in the spring and summer months. Twenty one percent of the attempted intercourse women and 25% of those who experienced attempted intercourse with violence reported that the male was under the influence of alcohol. Thirty six percent of these women told no one. Aggression was associated with more permanent relationships such as being pinned or going steady indicating sex exploitation resulting from emotional involvement.

2.13 Kanin, Eugene J.
1969 "Selected Dyadic Aspects of Male Sex Aggression." Journal of Sex Research 5:12-28.

Purpose: To examine the characteristics of aggressive-male and offended-female pairings in order to reveal that these relationships tend to have similar social and personal variables and do not occur randomly.

Method: The questionnaire was distributed and completed by a sample of 341 undergraduate university males. Sexually aggressive acts were defined by self reports of forceful attempts for coitus which were disagreeable or offensive to the woman, perceptions of female offended reactions, and description of the act.

Findings: 25.5 percent of the men reported perpetrating at least one sexually aggressive act since entering college. Offended reactions by victims were not random, but tended to be associated with the level of involvement in relationship. Sexual aggression has been found to occur at all stages in dating, but the results show that the majority of aggressive acts (60.8%) occurred in casual dating. The stage of the relationship at which men are sexually aggressive is significantly related to social class. Upper middle class men reported perpetrating more aggressive acts in stages of serious involvement, while working class men report perpetrating most acts during casual dating. Cross-sex communication failure appears to be associated with sexual aggression in the majority of offenses which were preceded by advanced consented sexual activity. Cross-class communication failure tends to increase the misunderstandings between men and women. In some situations, sexual aggressiveness appears to be used as a form of social control, a way for a man to force a woman whom he views to be deviant to follow the norms of dating. In these cases, retribution and punishment, rather than sex, are the motives. When a man believes that his partner is sexually promiscuous, whether true or not, chances increase that he will exhibit sexually aggressive behavior. Relationships involving sexual aggression tend to be more heterogamous in terms of religion, intelligence, status, age, education, fraternity-sorority membership than aggression-free relationships. Offended and nonoffended women did not differ significantly on male ratings of attractiveness. The study also reanalyzes characteristics of the aggressive-male and offended-female pairings comparing double standard men (those who believe that it is more wrong for a woman to engage in premarital sex than a man) and single standard men (believes premarital sex to be acceptable for both men and women).

2.14 Kanin, Eugene J. and Stanley R. Parcell
1977 "Sexual Aggression: A Second Look at the Offended Female." Archives of Sexual Behavior 6,1:67-76.

Purpose: The study measures the incidence of female's experiences of male sexual aggression and compares the findings to a similar study conducted during the 1950s.
Method: Two hundred and eighty two undergraduate females responded to a questionnaire that focused on their experiences with male sexual aggression. In addition, 55 females participated in group discussions on dating-courtship activities.
Findings: Approximately half of the sample population experienced sexual aggression, ranging from kissing to intercourse with violence. This finding is consistent with the earlier study. That data reveal that women had experienced these episodes during and prior to college. When looking at the sample's experience over time, 83% experienced some form of sexual aggression. A significant amount of the experiences of aggression were not preceded by consensual activity. For example, 36% of breast fondling were not preceded by consensual kissing and 54% of intercourse efforts were not preceded by consensual foreplay. In looking at women who experienced more serious forms of sexual aggression, they tended to be more sexually experienced and admitted to engaging in sexual aggression against males more than non-offended women. One of the most significant findings pertains to the victim offender relationship. In the earlier study, sexual aggression was more likely to occur in a steady dating relationship and the present study indicates the opposite. Women were more likely to be victimized in casual dating relationships.

2.15 Kirkpatrick, Clifford and Eugene Kanin
1957 "Male Sex Aggression on a University Campus." American Sociological Review 22:52-58.

Purpose: To understand the characteristics of male sexually aggressive behavior on a university campus.
Method: Data for the study were collected through a questionnaire which was distributed and completed by a sample of 291 female undergraduate students. Sexual aggressiveness was divided into five categories: attempts at "necking," "petting" above the waist, "petting" below the waist, sexual intercourse with threats or actual use of violence.
Findings: 55.7 percent of the women reported experiencing sexual aggression at least once during the academic year. 20.9 percent of the women experienced forceful attempts at intercourse and for 6.2 percent of these women, these attempts involved violence or threats of violence. Many of the women had been sexually assaulted more than once. When looking at time of year, the lesser offenses occur most often in the fall and the more severe offenses tend to occur most often in the spring. The authors attribute these findings to communication and involvement in relationships. The offended women tended to be younger, of a higher academic class, members of sororities, more religious, and go on dates significantly more than nonoffended women. However, the relationship between numbers of dates and the most severe offenses was not significant. There is a significant association between the seriousness of the offense and the stage in relationship. Less severe offenses tend to occur with non-involved relationships, while more severe offenses tend to occur in "pinned" or engagement relationships. These results are attributed to potential for misunderstandings and male exploitation of feminine involvement. Tolerance ratios, the frequency of repeated offenses by the same man, are computed and analyzed. The tolerance ratios were highest for offenses of medium seriousness. Varying level of emotional involvement is used to explain these findings. When considering emotional reactions of victims, anger was the most common reaction to less severe offenses and anger and fear were most common in attempted intercourse and attempted

intercourse with violence. Feelings of guilt were also found to vary with level of aggression. Analysis of reactions to offenses reveal that reactions vary according to level of aggression, but reliance on authority in consistently low.

2.16 Korman, Sheila and Gerald Leslie
1982 "The Relationship of Feminist Ideology and Date Expense Sharing to Perceptions of Sexual Aggression in Dating." Journal of Sex Research 18,2:114-129.

Purpose: The study compares the incidence of sexual aggression between an undergraduate population in 1982 and the population surveyed by Kanin and Parcell (1977) in 1971-72. Additionally, women's adherence to feminist ideology and sharing of dating experiences are examined.
Method: Four hundred undergraduate students responded to questionnaires that measured feminist ideology, experiences of sexual aggression, and date expense sharing.
Findings: Sixty-three percent of the participants indicated that they had experienced offensive male sexual aggression on dates during their senior year of high school. Kanin and Parcell (1977) reported that half of their sample had been offended at some level of erotic intimacy. Since high school, participants experienced less episodes of sexual aggression but the episodes that they experienced were more coitally directed. The data indicate no relationship between adherence to feminist ideology and the occurrence of sexual aggression. However, date expense sharing had a significant relationship to sexual aggression. Women who shared dating expenses were more likely to experience sexual aggression than women whose date paid. Women who hold feminist attitudes were significantly more likely to participate in date expense sharing than women who had traditional values. This finding has important ramifications for women who hold feminist values.

2.17 Koss, Mary P.

1985 "The Hidden Rape Victim: Personality, Attitudinal, and Situational Characteristics." Psychology of Women Quarterly 9:193-212.

Purpose: The study identifies hidden rape victims and tests social control, victim precipitation, and situational blame models to determine victimization status.
Method: Female undergraduate students were selected from their responses to the Sexual Experiences Survey (Koss and Oros, 1982). The sample represented five victimization categories: not sexually victimized, low sexual victimization; moderate sexual victimization; high sexual victimization and acknowledged their sexual victimization; and high sexual victimization and did not acknowledge sexual victimization. Subjects participated in a one on one interview where they completed the SES and questionnaires that measured victim precipitation, social control, and situational blame models.
Findings: Thirty-eight percent of the respondents had experiences that met the legal definition of rape and only 4% labeled their experiences as rape. Both personality and attitudinal factors failed to distinguish the types of victims. However, the situational factors indicate that low and moderate sexual victimization subjects experienced less offender force and they resisted more than high sexual victimization subjects. Unacknowledged rapes were more likely to take place within the context of a dating relationship. In these situations, the close relationship and shared intimacy disqualified the experience as rape in the victim's mind.

2.18 Koss, Mary

1988 "Hidden Rape: Sexual Aggression and Victimization in a National Sample of Students in Higher Education." Pp. 3-26 in Rape and Sexual Assault II, edited by Ann Wolbert Burgess. New York: Garland Publishing.

Purpose: To obtain more accurate rates of prevalence and

incidence of rape than those provided by official crime statistics such as the Uniform Crime Reports and National Crime Survey. Method: Part of the Ms. Magazine Project on Campus Sexual Assault, 6159 students enrolled in 32 institutions of higher education in the United States answered self-report questionnaires. Findings: Prevalence of sexual victimization: 53.7% of women reported some form of sexual victimization. The most serious form of aggression experiences by women were: sexual contact: 14.4%, sexual coercion: 11.9%, attempted rape: 12.1%, and rape: 15.4%. Rates of sexual victimization differed significantly by region, governance of institution, and ethnicity but not by size of city or institution, type of institution, or minority enrollment. Prevalence of sexual aggression: 25.1% of men reported perpetrating some form of sexual aggression. The most extreme forms perpetrated were: sexual contact: 10.2%, sexual coercion: 7.2%, attempted rape: 3.3%, and rape: 4.4%. Rates of reported sexual aggression differed by region and ethnicity. Descriptive profile of sexual victimization: Some of the findings include: Rapes happened between the ages of 18 and 19. 84% of victims knew their rapist. The rapes mostly happened off campus. Prior intimacy had generally occurred, but victims believed that they made their nonconsent quite clear. The offender, typically, used "quite a bit" of force such as twisting arms or holding down. Women reported that they resisted a moderate amount with reasoning and physical force. Victims felt scared, angry, and depressed during assault. They felt somewhat responsible, but believed that offenders were more responsible. Almost half of the victims did not report the rape to anyone. Of the small percentage who did report the crime, most found the police to be unsupportive and family and crisis centers to be supportive. Descriptive profile of sexual aggression: Perpetrators reported much of the same information as victims: 84% knew their victims, most rapes occurred off campus, and they reported being "somewhat" forceful. However, offenders generally felt proud during assault. They felt vaguely responsible but believed that their victims were equally or more responsible. 47% of men who raped reported that they expect to do it again. 88% of men whose acts met the legal definition of rape adamantly denied that the acts were rape.

This work has become the standard by which other incidence studies are judged. It provided the first large scale, multi-institution measurement of sexual aggression among college students.

2.19 Koss, Mary
1992 "The Underdetection of Rape: Methodological Choices Influence Incidence Estimates." Journal of Social Issues 14,1:61-75.

Purpose: To discuss the incidence and extent of rape in the United States, and present a critical analysis of current methods of estimating rape incidence.
Method: Review of Literature
Findings: Federal data sources make use of flawed definitions of rape; they also limit disclosure of rape, the UCR by including only those reported to police and the NCS by limiting confidentiality and context of the interviews. In the U.S., far more women are raped than is reported, and rapes are more likely to involve acquaintances. A review of independent data sources reveals an incidence of rape 6-10 times higher than reported by the National Crime Survey. Evidence to support a rape "epidemic" is currently inconclusive.

2.20 Koss, Mary; Thomas Dinero; Cynthia Seibel; and Susan Cox
1988 "Stranger and Acquaintance Rape: Are There Differences in Victim's Experience." Psychology of Women Quarterly 12:1-24.

Purpose: The study compares the experiences of stranger and acquaintance rape victims. Specific attention is focused on the number of episodes experienced, victim's resistance, victim's perceptions of their rape experiences, and psychological symptoms.
Method: Participants were chosen based on their responses to a self reported questionnaire that was administered to 6,159 students

at 32 U.S. institutions of higher learning. Sexual victimization was determined by responses to the Sexual Experiences Survey (1982). Four hundred and eighty nine women identified that they had had experiences that met the legal definition of rape. For the purposes of this study, they were categorized as either stranger or acquaintance rape victims. Acquaintance rape victims were classified into groups based on their relationship with the offender: nonromantic acquaintance, a casual date, a steady date, and a family member.

Findings: Stranger rape victims rated the offender as more aggressive, reported higher degrees of fear, and felt that the offender was more responsible for what happened. Stranger rapes were also more likely to involve threats of bodily harm, hitting and slapping, and a weapon. On the other hand, acquaintance rapes were more likely to involve only one offender and to have been perpetrated several times by the same offender. Approximately half of both groups indicated that they were drinking before the assault, but more stranger rape victims reported using alcohol and drugs before the assault. Stranger rape victims were more likely to discuss the assault with some one and to have reported their assault to the police. They also sought crisis services more frequently than acquaintance rape victims. The two groups did not differ significantly according to psychological symptoms and victim resistance.

The four acquaintance rape groups differed significantly in their perceptions of the rape. Offender aggression including hitting and slapping, choking and beating, and displaying a weapon were most common among victims assaulted by family members. The more serious the relationship between the victim and offender, the less likely the victim was to tell anyone about the assault.

2.21 Koss, Mary and Christine A. Gidycz

1985 "Sexual Experiences Survey: Reliability and Validity." Journal of Consulting and Clinical Psychology 53,3:422-423.

Purpose: In this study, the researchers develop an instrument that is capable of measuring the experiences of those rape victims who do not report their experiences to the police or university officials.
Method: Undergraduate students responded to the Sexual Experiences Survey, a 12 item survey regarding their experiences with various degrees of coercion and forces associated with sexual intercourse.
Findings: More people are experiencing sexual victimization than is known by the authorities. These people are referred to as "hidden victims." The instrument was both valid and reliable. Women who have experienced rape responded consistently whether the instrument was administered in private or with an interviewer. There was a tendency among males to deny behaviors in interviews that had been revealed on self-reports.

2.22 Koss, Mary; Christine A. Gidycz; and Nadine Wisniewski
1987 "The Scope of Rape: Incidence and Prevalence of Sexual Aggression and Victimization in a National Sample of Higher Education Students." Journal of Consulting and Clinical Psychology 55,2:162-170.

Purpose: The study measures the incidence of sexual aggression in institutions of higher learning in the United States.
Method: Undergraduate students, 6,159, from 32 institutions of higher learning responded to the Sexual Experiences Survey. The population represented a diverse group of individuals based on race, religion, and gender.
Findings: 53.7% of the women indicated that they had experienced some form of sexual victimization. Of these women, 14.4% experienced unwanted sexual contact, 11.9% sexual coercion, 12% attempted rape, and 15.4% completed rape. Twenty-five percent of the men revealed involvement in some form of sexual aggression. The prevalence of sexual victimization did not vary according to the size of the city where the institution was located, the size of the institution, or by minority enrollment. However, sexual victimization rates did differ according to the institution's region of the country and type of institution.

Victimization rates were slightly higher in the Great Lakes and Plains States than in other regions. Men admitted rape twice as often in the Southwest as in the Plains States and three times as often as men in the West. Women in private schools and major universities experienced double the rate of victimization of women in public non-major institutions. Native American women experienced the highest rates of sexual victimization followed by White, Black, Hispanic, and Asian women. Similarly the number of men who perpetrated sexual victimization varied by ethnic group. Black men expressed the highest rates of sexual aggression followed by Hispanic, White, Asian, and Native American men. The study reveals that rape on campus is much more prevalent than once believed.

2.23 Koss, Mary and Cheryl J. Oros
1982 "Sexual Experiences Survey: A Research Instrument Investigating Sexual Aggression and Victimization." Journal of Consulting and Clinical Psychology 50,3:455-457.

Purpose: The researchers develop an instrument to measure experiences of rape victims who do not report to the police or university officials.
Method: Undergraduate students, 1846 male and 2016 females, responded to the Sexual Experiences Survey, a twelve-item yes/no response survey regarding various degrees of coercion and force associated with sexual intercourse.
Findings: The results indicate that more women are experiencing sexual victimization than are known to the authorities. These women are referred to as "hidden victims" and it is suggested that this instrument is useful in identifying them.

This instrument, and variations on it, have become well-known and widely used in the research on acquaintance and date rape.

2.24 Lane, Katherine E. and Patricia A. Gwartney-Gibbs
1985 "Violence in the Context of Dating and Sex." Journal of Family Issues 6,1:45-69.

Purpose: This study uses a broader definition of dating and courting relationships to examine incidence and demographic variables.
Method: Mail-out/mail-back questionnaires were sent to a random sample of university undergraduates, obtaining a 55.5% response rate. Courtship/relationship variables were expanded to include more casual dating experiences and a broader time reference.
Findings: They reported a higher incidence of courtship violence than previous studies, finding nearly one-third of the respondents reporting either inflicting or receiving the threat of violence. 25% of females reported having sex when they didn't want to due to verbal coercion. Females reported higher receiving more threats (5.3%) and experiencing more violence (12.9%) from men to coerce sex.

2.25 Lundberg-Love, Paula and Robert Geffner
1989 "Date Rape: Prevalence, Risk Factors, and a Proposed Model." Pp. 169-84 in Violence in Dating Relationships, edited by Maureen Pirog-Good and Jan Stets. New York: Praeger.

Purpose: To discuss the prevalence and risk factors of date rape and incorporate them into a Four-Preconditions Model of Date Rape.
Method: Theoretical model construction
Findings: Discusses risk factors for date rape which have been identified in past research including control issues, communication and interpretation, alcohol use, location and activity, and sex-role attitudes. Introduces childhood or adolescent incest as another potential risk factor. Applies these risk factors to Finkelhor's four factor model of sexual abuse and develops a Four-Preconditions Model of Date Rape. Provides policy implications and practice.

2.26 Miller, Beverly and Jon C. Marshall.
1987 "Coercive Sex on the University Campus." Journal of College Student Personnel 28:38-47.

Purpose: To study the prevalence of coercive sex and date rape on university campuses, the accompanying physical force and psychological pressures, and gender differences in perception of these pressures.
Method: Questionnaires were distributed and completed by 795 undergraduate and graduate students at two universities. The Sexual Experience Survey was used to gather data on sexual experiences at the university, sexual experiences prior to coming to the university, and background information.
Findings: Psychological pressures: Twenty-five percent of women reported being coerced into sex by psychological pressure and fifteen percent of men reported using psychological pressure to coerce women into having sex. Psychological pressures included statements of uncontrollable sexual arousal, threats to end relationship, continual arguing, and lying. The most common pressures experienced by women were arguments of uncontrollable sexual arousal (15%) and continual arguments (17%). Men most often reported saying things they did not mean in order to coerce women (30%). Physical force: Fourteen percent of women reported being physically forced to kiss or pet. Two percent of men reported using physical force during these acts. Two percent of women reported being physical force to engage in sexual intercourse while less than one percent of men reported using physical force during sex. Two percent of women reported being coerced into oral or anal sex through physical force while less than two percent of men reported using physical force during these acts. Sixty percent of women and eleven percent of men who had experienced coercive sex reported being under the influence of alcohol and drugs. According to both women and men, most acts of coercive sex occurred in a private home or apartment. Sixty-six percent of the women told someone about the assault and twenty-seven percent received medical assistance. Most of the men were not aware of these actions. Although their experiences and actions

meet legal definitions of rape, most women and men did not define their experiences and actions as date rape.

2.27 Mills, Crystal S. and Barbara J. Granoff.
1992 "Date and Acquaintance Rape among a Sample of College Students." Social Work 37,6:504-509.

Purpose: To examine the prevalence of sexual assaults at the University of Hawaii - Manoa and analyze the relationship between reported assaults and ethnicity.
Method: As part of a needs-assessment program, questionnaires were distributed and completed by 219 students in English classes at the University of Hawaii, Manoa. Women were asked about personal victimization experiences and men were asked about personal perpetration experiences.
Findings: Victims: Twenty-eight percent of the women reported being victims of rape or attempted rape. Caucasian and Japanese women experienced the most sexual victimization of all forms. Seventy-seven percent of the women know their attacker. Fifteen percent of the women who were raped and forty percent who were victims of attempted rape told someone about the assault. Only one women who experienced an attempted rape, however, reported it to the police. Of the women who had a relationship with the perpetrator before the assault, 45 percent reported that the relationship continued afterwards. Perpetrators: One out of six men reported perpetrating acts that met the Hawaiian legal definition of sexual assault. However, only 1.9 percent of the men reported perpetrating rape and 8.5 reported perpetrating attempted rape. Many more admitted to perpetrating other types of sexually aggressive behavior such as continuing to make sexual advances after partner said no (29.2%). Most men (97.2%) responded that they would not force sex even if they thought they could get away with it. However, 10.4 percent of the men believed that women want them to be forceful and 50.9 percent believed that when women say no they sometimes mean yes. Caucasian and Japanese men reported perpetrating sexual assaults more than men of other ethnic groups.

2.28 Muehlenhard, Charlene L. and Polly L. Falcon
1990 "Men's Heterosocial Skill and Attitudes Toward Women as Predictors of Verbal Sexual Coercion and Forceful Rape." Sex Roles 23,5/6:241-259

Purpose: Tests the hypothesis that heterosocially skilled men will be more likely to engage in verbal sexual coercion, while unskilled men will be more likely to engage in physical coercion, given that both accept traditional gender roles or male sexual dominance.
Method: The Survey of Heterosexual Interactions and the Sexual Experiences Survey were given to 1152 male undergraduates. Scales were also used to measure Sexist Attitudes Toward Women, Sex Role Stereotyping, Adversarial Sexual Beliefs, and Acceptance of Interpersonal Violence.
Findings: Physical coercion was seen as part of a general pattern of sexual coercion. Rapists were more likely to advocate traditional gender roles and male sexual dominance. Lower heterosexual skills did not relate significantly to the likelihood to commit acts of coercion. The hypothesized interaction was not found.

2.29 Murnen, Sarah K.; Annette Perot; and Donn Byrne
1989 "Coping with Unwanted Sexual Activity: Normative Responses, Situational Determinants, and Individual Differences." Journal of Sex Research 26,1:85-106.

Purpose: The study examines women's reactions to unwanted sexual attention, including normative and individual coping strategies.
Method: One hundred and thirty undergraduate women responded to a questionnaire that measured the following variables: demographics, unwanted sexual activity, coping mechanisms, self esteem, locus of control, sexual opinions, rape myth acceptance, submissive sexual fantasies, and importance of romantic relationships and sexuality.

Findings: Over half of the sample indicated that they had experienced unwanted sexual activity during the past two years. The majority of the experiences were with someone whom they knew fairly well. Their experiences ranged from unwanted kissing to intercourse. The most common response to the unwanted behavior, regardless of what it was, was to respond with nothing or a strong verbal response. In general, women indicated that they felt that they had a significant amount of control over dealing with unwanted sex. However, coping variables were not related to responses. Situational variables were the best predictors of women's responses. The findings suggest that those women who experienced unwanted sexual activity had little ability to deal with them. This indicates a need for men and women to learn how to communicate with their sexual partners.

2.30 Parrot, Andrea and Laurie Bechhofer
1991 Acquaintance Rape: The Hidden Crime. New York: John Wiley.

Purpose: To make scholarly work on acquaintance rape available to practitioners who work outside of academia.
Method: Review of literature.
Findings: The volume summarizes an extensive literature on acquaintance rape in chapters by various experts in the field. Chapters present empirical findings regarding various aspects of acquaintance rape, as well as practical suggestions for educators and clinicians. Chapters include reports of empirical studies of rape myths, attitudes about acquaintance rape, factors contributing to acquaintance rape, types of acquaintance rape, victim characteristics, assailants, effects of acquaintance rape, societal response, and prevention. See entries in this volume under Abbey; Bechhofer and Parrot; Bohmer; Burkhart; Burt; Calhoun; Gidycz and Koss; Harney and Muehlenhard; Katz; Malamuth and Dean; Mandoki and Burkhart; Muehlenhard; O'Sullivan; Parrot; Rapaport and Posey; Richardson and Hammock; Rozee, Bateman, and Gilmore; Russell; Struckman-Johnson; Warshaw and Parrot; White and Humphrey.

2.31 Rivera, George and Robert Regoli
1987 "Sexual Victimization Experiences of Sorority Women." Sociology and Social Research 72:39-42.

Purpose: To report on a study of the incidence and prevalence of sexual assault among sorority women at a large southwestern university.
Method: A mail questionnaire was sent to a sample of women in sororities on campus. The response rate was 43.5%.
Findings: Over half of the respondents had experienced forced touching of their intimate parts; thirty-five percent had experience attempted penetration, and seventeen percent had experienced assault with penetration. The authors conclude that sexual assault is common among sorority women.

2.32 Russell, Diana E. H.
1984 Sexual Exploitation: Rape, Child Sexual Abuse, and Workplace Harassment. Beverly Hills, CA: Sage.

Purpose: Parts 1 and 2 of this review book are devoted to the subject of rape.
Method: Research Review.
Findings: Chapter 1 is especially relevant to the topic of acquaintance rape as it compares the rape rates derived from studies using a wide range of methodologies, and demonstrates that rapes by acquaintances are likely to be undercounted in "official" sources versus confidential self-reports. The remainder of Part 1 is a review of social and psychological characteristics of victims and perpetrators. In Part 2, a variety of factors conducive to rape are considered, including pornography, gender socialization, and gender stratification.

2.33 Sorenson, Susan B.; Judith A. Stein; Judith M. Siegel; Jacqueline M. Golding; and M. Audrey Burnham

1987 "The Prevalence of Adult Sexual Assault: The Los Angeles Epidemiologic Catchment Area Project." American Journal of Epidemiology 126,6:1154-1164.

Purpose: To present a large-scale, population-based study of sexual assault, to estimate prevalence and type. It differs from most studies in that it is attempting a more generalizable estimate than one can draw from a university population.

Method: The sample was 3,132 adults from two LA catchment areas, one predominately Hispanic (83%), the other predominately non-Hispanic (63%). Respondents were interviewed in person, then by telephone six months later, then personally a year later, as part of the Los Angeles Epidemiologic Catchment Area Project. Along with the mental health questions, respondents were asked about lifetime sexual assault experiences. Sexual assault was defined as sexual contact by pressure or force. Respondents answering affirmatively were asked further questions concerning specifics (age, type of force, type of activity, etc.)

Findings: Findings for adult sexual assault and lifetime sexual assault were reported. The findings on childhood sexual assault were presented in another paper. 10.5% of all those surveyed reported adult sexual assault. By gender, 7.2% of the male and 13.5% of females reported such. Hispanics reported 6.8% while non-white Hispanics reported 15.5%. The highest rates were reported by non-Hispanic females 18-39 years (26.3%), although overall, significant effects were found for sex only. Of those reporting sexual assaults two-thirds reported two or more. In 78.5% of the most recent assaults the respondent knew the attacker. More than one-fourth of the perpetrators were the spouse or lover of the victim. Older respondents reported less sexual assault than younger ones.

2.34 Stets, Jan E. and Maureen A. Pirog-Good.
1989 "Patterns of Physical and Sexual Abuse for Men and Women in Dating Relationships: A Descriptive Analysis." Journal of Family Violence 4,1:63-76.

Purpose: To contribute to research on abuse in dating relationships by using retrospective data that allows for analysis of physical and sexual abuse of men and women in up to four dating relationships. Examination of the extent to which dating abuse in one relationship is independent of abuse in other relationships. Understanding of help-seeking patterns of victims.
Method: A sample of 118 men and 169 women undergraduate college students completed a questionnaire containing questions on physical and sexual dating abuse. Sexual abuse was measured by asking if subjects sustained any one of eight increasingly severe types of assaults against their will with any of their last four dating partners. Only the results concerning sexual abuse will be discussed in this abstract.
Findings: Twenty-two percent of the men and 36% of the women reported sustaining sexual abuse by one or more dating partners. Women reported more incidents of sexual abuse than physical abuse. Both men and women appear to be more likely to sustain less severe forms of sexual abuse. Women who sustained sexual abuse dated significantly more than women who did not. For men, there was not a significant difference in the amount of dating. When considering the independence of abusive relationships, it was found that women were twice as likely as expected to be sexually abused under the assumption of independence across relationships. Men, however, were not significantly more likely than expected to sustain sexual abuse under the assumption of independence. Physical and sexual abuse are associated for women, but not for men. Thus, women are more likely than men to experience physical and sexual abuse in the same relationship. Only about 40% of the men and women who sustained sexual abuse perceived their relationships as abusive. Thus, perceptions and experiences of abuse are often different. Women and men were most likely to report abusive acts

to friends. However, women were significantly more likely to do so. None of the men and only seven percent of the women reported the assaults to criminal justice authorities. Suggestions for prevention and future research are provided.

2.35 Ward, Sally; Kathy Chapman; Ellen Cohn; Susan White; and Kirk Williams
1991 "Acquaintance Rape and the College Social Scene." Family Relations 40:65-71.

Purpose: To discuss the methodological and conceptual problems in the literature on acquaintance rape and to present the results of a study of the incidence of rape on one particular campus.
Method: The study used survey research administered to a sample of students on one campus. The sample was constructed by sampling courses and administering the survey to all students in the courses selected to be in the study. The sample includes 524 women and 337 men.
Findings: 34% of the women respondents reported they had experienced unwanted sexual contact; 20% reported unwanted attempted sexual intercourse; and 10% reported unwanted sexual intercourse. Detailed reports about the most serious incident experienced show that the experiences occurred often in residences, they were party-related, and they usually involve alcohol use. Important differences were found between incidents involving the woman's "boyfriend" and those involving an "acquaintance." "Stranger" assaults did occur, but these were not strangers in the stereotypical sense; rather, these assaults occurred in the context of the "normal" social scene on campus, usually during or after parties in fraternities or dorms.

2.36 Warshaw, Robin
1988 I Never Called it Rape: The Ms. Report on Recognizing, Fighting and Surviving Date and Acquaintance Rape. New York: Harper and Row.

Purpose: To present the findings of the Ms. Report on Date and

Acquaintance Rape to the general public. More details on method and findings are reported under works by M. Koss in this bibliography.

Method: Questionnaires and personal interviews. See works by M. Koss for more details.

Findings: Findings from the Koss national survey on acquaintance rape are combined with personal interviews with acquaintance rape survivors. One in four female respondents had an experience that met the legal definition of rape or attempted rape. Of the women whose sexual assault met the legal definition of rape, only 27% thought of themselves as rape victims. Forty-two percent of the rape victims told no one about their assaults; 5% reported to the police; and only 5% sought help at a rape crisis center. One in twelve male students said that they had committed acts that met the legal definition of rape or attempted rape. Sixteen percent of the male students who committed rape and 10% of those who attempted rape took part in episodes involving more than one perpetrator.

3

SOCIAL CORRELATES OF ACQUAINTANCE RAPE

3.1 Abbey, Antonia
1991 "Acquaintance Rape and Alcohol Consumption on College Campuses: How Are They Linked?" Journal of American College Health 39:165-169.

Purpose: Examines the link between heavy drinking and high incidence of acquaintance rape on college campuses, directed toward encouraging future research and program development. No empirical observations are reported, but the author outlines seven possible explanations for the relationship between alcohol and date rape, three focusing on the perpetrator and four focusing upon the victim. These are outlined below. Policy and program suggestions are presented, with some indications of the focus of future research.

Summary: Expectancies about alcohol's effects--Men expect to feel stronger, more powerful, sexual and aggressive after drinking. These beliefs can lead to behavior that seeks to fulfill them, leading to verbal or physical confrontations, or the creation of a sexual one.

Misperceptions of sexual intent--Men are more likely to interpret cues and signals more sexually than women. The use of alcohol is likely to increase the probability of this misinterpretation.

Alcohol consumption as justification--Some statutes and jurors, as well as perpetrators, view intoxication as justification for behavior. In general, it justifies many forms of acting out, including using women as sexual objects.

Alcohol's effect on the ability of women to send and receive cues--High levels of consumption may cause women to ignore or simply miss indications that an assault may occur. Men have been shown to interpret friendly behavior as seduction. When intoxicated, this may not be noticed and rectified.

Alcohol's effect on women's ability to resist sexual assault--Evidence suggests that prompt action may prevent some assaults. Alcohol impairs cognitive and motor ability to do this.

Stereotypes about women who consume alcohol--"Women who drink are perceived as sexually available." Men may encourage drinking in order to facilitate an assault.

Women's enhanced sense of responsibility--"Women who were drunk when raped are often viewed by others as partially responsible." This may reflect a perceived failure in the "gatekeeper" role of traditional sex-stereotypes.

3.2 Boeringer, Scot B.; Constance L. Shehan; and Ronald L. Akers

1991 "Social Contexts and Social Learning in Sexual Coercion and Aggression: Assessing the Contribution of Fraternity Membership." Family Relations 40:58-64.

Purpose: To apply social learning theory of deviant behavior to explain sexual coercion and aggression among fraternity members. Method: A questionnaire was distributed and completed by 262 undergraduate men. Data were collected on fraternity membership, differential association (measured by two questions asking the extent to which friends engage in sexual aggression), differential reinforcement (measured using three questions asking about the extent to which their friends approve of sexual promiscuity and aggression), definitions (measured using Burt's 1980 scale of myths and supports for rape), and modeling (measured through questions about the exposure to media containing sexually violent depictions).

Findings: Fraternity members and nonmembers did not different significantly on background characteristics including age, race, grade point average, educational goals, and political and religious beliefs. Thus, there is not support for the argument that differences in sexual aggressive behavior between fraternity members and nonmembers is a result of differences in background characteristics. Fraternity members and nonmembers did not differ significantly in terms of self-perceived likelihood of sexual aggression or reports of rape, but fraternity members were significantly more likely to report using nonphysical force and drugs or alcohol to obtain sex. In addition, fraternity members differed significantly from nonmembers in terms of differential association and differential reinforcement. Fraternity members were more likely to associate with men who engage in sexually aggressive behavior and to be reinforced by their friends when being sexually coercive or aggressive. Multivariate analysis results reveal that when the effects of social learning variables are controlled, fraternity membership does not have a significant effect on self-perceived likelihood of sexual aggression, use of drugs or alcohol, nonphysical coercion, or physical force to obtain sex. Thus, the relationships between fraternity membership and sexual coercion and aggression can be attributed to significant differences between fraternity members and nonmembers in aspects of social learning theory and the study finds support for using social learning theory to understand sexual aggression and coercion among fraternity members. Implications for intervention are discussed.

3.3 Burke, Peter; Jan E. Stets; and Maureen A. Pirog-Good
1988 "Gender Identity, Self-Esteem, and Physical and Sexual Abuse in Dating Relationships." Social Psychology Quarterly 51:272-285.

Purpose: To examine the relationship between gender identity, self esteem and other characteristics and inflicting and sustaining physical and sexual abuse in dating relationships. Only the results concerning sexual abuse are discussed in this abstract.

Method: The study is based on a sample of 505 (298 women and 207 men) college students. A questionnaire was used to the collect data. Sexual abuse was measured by asking students to indicate the number of times they inflicted or sustained sexual acts against their partner's or their own will. Gender identity was determined using a measure developed by Burke and Tully and self-esteem was measured using Rosenberg's self esteem scale. Data were also collected regarding acceptance of aggression, behavioral involvement in the relationship, and childhood experiences with abuse.

Findings: Men reported inflicting sexual abuse significantly more frequently than women and women reported sustaining sexual abuse significantly more frequently than men. Gender identity and inflicting. For men, gender identity is directly related to infliction of sexual abuse. The less masculine the men, the more likely they are to inflict sexual abuse. Gender identity of women has indirect effects on infliction of sexual abuse through behavioral involvement and acceptance of aggression. Self esteem and inflicting. For both men and women, self esteem was not directly related to infliction of sexual abuse. Other variables. For both men and women, behavioral involvement was and acceptance of aggression was not significantly related to inflicting sexual abuse. Gender identity and sustaining. Gender identity of men had significant direct and indirect effects on sustaining sexual abuse. Again, the less masculine the men, the more likely they were to sustain sexual abuse. For women, gender identity has an indirect effect on sustaining sexual abuse through behavioral involvement and self-esteem. For women also, the less masculine the gender identity, the more likely they are to sustain sexual abuse. Self esteem and sustaining. Women's self esteem is directly related to sustaining sexual abuse, but self esteem has no direct effect on sustaining sexual abuse for men. Other variables. For men, sustaining sexual abuse is related to witnessing and experiencing abuse in childhood, behavioral involvement, and acceptance of aggression. For women, behavioral involvement and experiencing abuse as children are related to sustaining sexual abuse. The authors explain their findings regarding gender identity as a possible result of differences between masculine and feminine orientations to dating relationships.

3.4 Gwartney-Gibbs, Patricia and Jean Stockard
1989 "Courtship Aggression and Mixed-Sex Peer Groups." Pp. 185-204 in Violence in Dating Relationships, edited by Maureen Pirog-Good and Jan Stets. New York: Praeger.

Purpose: To replicate a 1982 study which found that it is possible to identify distinct subgroups of college students according to experiences with sexual aggression in dating relationships and compare the results.
Method: A random sample of 485 undergraduates at a public university received mail, self administered questionnaires. The dependent variable is peer group membership. Independent variables included courtship violence (1982 only), demographic characteristics, college characteristics, certain values, attitudes, and behaviors.
Findings: Again, three distinct peer groups emerged: nonaggressive (neither male friends who were sexually aggressive or female friends who were had been victims), female victimization (had female friends who had been victims, but not sexually aggressive male friends), aggressive peer group (had both female friends who had been victims and sexually aggressive male friends). Only 1% of students for both studies were described as having sexually aggressive male friends, but no female friends who had been victimized. The proportion of students in the nonaggressive group remained the same in the replicated study. However, there were approximately a 10% increase in the female victimization peer group and a 13% decrease in the sexually aggressive peer group. These changes were statistically significant. Females in the sexually aggressive group were more likely than others to report inflicting both violence and sexual violence and to report sustaining sexual violence. There is no difference in parental aggression of men or women between the peer groups. After considering many demographic and college characteristics including race, religion, amount of spending money,

parents' education, G.P.A, living arrangements, and major, the peer groups show statistically significant differences only in education orientation and use of alcohol and drugs. Differing from the 1982 study, the best predictor of peer group membership for men is being a social student. Use of alcohol and drugs, educational aspirations, major, year in school also had influences. For women, the best predictors are living arrangements, year in school, race/ethnicity, and religious affiliation. Alcohol consumption, being a serious student, and academic major had moderate influence.

3.5 Harney, Patricia A. and Charlene L. Muehlenhard
1991 "Factors that Increase the Likelihood of Victimization." Pp.159-75 in Acquaintance Rape: The Hidden Crime, edited by Andrea Parrot and Laurie Bechhofer. New York: John Wiley and Sons.

Purpose: To review research on the cultural, situational, and personal characteristics that are associated with increased likelihood of being victimized by rape. The emphasis is on acquaintance rape, but not exclusively so.
Method: Review of literature.
Findings: The cultural ideology of male dominance and support for intergroup and interpersonal violence are more prevalent in societies with higher rape rates. Within cultures, individuals with greater acceptance of traditional gender-role norms are more accepting of rape myths and rape-conducive attitudes. Media violence and pornography are possible means by which rape-conducive cultural beliefs are communicated. Situational factors that arc linked to victimization include dating rituals in which the man initiates, pays, and provides the transportation for the date. Additional situational factors are the number of dating and sexual partners a woman has had and her past level of sexual activity. More research is needed to identify the causal factors accounting for these correlations. Victim-offender relationship and alcohol use are also associated with victimization; women are much more likely to be victimized by an acquaintance than by a stranger, and

alcohol use by the victim and perpetrator is prevalent. Some personal characteristics may also increase the likelihood of victimization; research on demographic factors, belief systems, and child sexual abuse is reviewed. Few consistent patterns are found for demographics and beliefs; recent research has shown an association between the experience of abuse as a child and revictimization as an adult. The authors conclude that the most general and effective way to reduce victimization is to equalize the power differential between men and women.

3.6 Koss, Mary and Thomas E. Dinero
1989 "Discriminant Analysis of Risk Factors for Sexual Victimization Among a National Sample of College Women." Journal of Consulting and Clinical Psychology 57,2: 242-250.

Purpose: To examine how accurately rape and lesser sexual assaults were predicted among a national sample of women. The study used a three-part vulnerability hypothesis, testing the vulnerability-creating potential of traumatic experiences, social-psychological variables, and vulnerability enhancing situations.
Method: The sample consisted of 3,187 college women, mean age 21.4 years. In this study, the authors analyzed the data only from the responses of the 2,723 white subjects. Data were gathered using a self-report questionnaire of 330 items divided into seven sections. Four variables developed from the questionnaire corresponded to the hypotheses mentioned above, vulnerability-creating traumatic situations, social-psychological variables, sexual attitudes, and vulnerability-enhancing situations.
Findings: All of the hypotheses had similar levels of predictive power and accuracy. Only the variables that reflected traumatic experiences identified rape victims at a rate that clearly improved prediction. A composite model of the six most discriminating variables correctly identified the sexual victimization level of half of the women including one-quarter of the rape victims. The authors suggested that "the individual vulnerability hypotheses were not as powerful alone as they were when the risk variables

were considered in association with one another." Another composite model, with variables for sexual abuse, sexual attitudes, alcohol use, and sexual activity, was demonstrated as representing almost all of the discriminating power. The variables had the most predictive power when coupled with alcohol use. The authors conclude that alcohol as a risk factor should be researched more thoroughly.

3.7 Levine, Edward M. and Kanin, Eugene J.
1987 "Sexual Violence Among Dates and Acquaintances: Trends and Their Implications for Marriage and Family." Journal of Family Violence 2,1:55-65.

Purpose: This review paper describes social changes occurring over the 1970s and early 1980s which may be related to apparent increases in sexual violence during that period.
Method: Research Review
Findings: Changes in traditional sex-role standards for men and women, such as the introduction of the contraceptive pill and increased female labor force participation and economic independence, may be related to increases in rape rates. Such changes have resulted in greater sexual and social freedom for women, but at the same time have led to a breakdown of the traditional forces which protected women. Other social changes include the increased acceptability of explicit sexual themes in the mass media (including pornography), and higher rates of drinking among adolescents and young adults. Rape is likely to lead to low self-esteem, sexual dysfunction, a lack of trust, and emotional disorders, all of which can adversely affect the well-being of victims and the families they subsequently form.

3.8 Makepeace, James
1986 "Gender Differences in Courtship Violence Victimization." Family Relations 35: 383-388.

Purpose: The author examined gender differences in the commission and experience of courtship violence, in the motives for such violence, and in perceptions of the effects of such violence.
Method: Incident data on 391 cases of courtship violence were obtained from a survey of 2338 undergraduates which focused on dating experiences. (NOTE: Most of this article is about physical violence; only findings relevant to date rape are discussed here.)
Findings: Females were much more likely (8 X) than males to indicate that forced sex had been attempted in course of their relationship. Women also were more likely to report being injured or emotionally harmed. The results suggest that there may be important gender differences in perceptions of the frequency, severity, and consequences of dating violence.

3.9 Mandoki, Catalina A. and Barry R. Burkhart
1991 "Women as Victims: Antecedents and Consequences of Acquaintance Rape." Pp.176-91 in Acquaintance Rape: The Hidden Crime, edited by Andrea Parrot and Laurie Bechhofer. New York: John Wiley and Sons.

Purpose: To review work on the antecedents and consequences of acquaintance rape victimization. This review is similar to the review in the same volume by Harney and Muehlenhard on the antecedents of acquaintance rape. It is unique in the discussion of consequences.
Method: Review of literature.
Findings: The antecedents of acquaintance rape are varied. The cultural beliefs supporting and legitimizing violence contribute to victimization. Childhood sexual abuse is also related to later victimization. Women's interaction skills are also important; women who are passive and less clear in communicating their

preferences in sexual interactions are more likely to be victimized than are more assertive women. The consequences of acquaintance rape include guilt, anxiety, and poor social and family adjustment. These consequences are long-term and distressing. The authors conclude with a caution that work on victimization offers a very incomplete picture at best of acquaintance rape. Work on the cultural context and on the dynamics of perpetration are crucial for a full view. Much more work is needed on the evaluation of prevention programs as well.

3.10 McCahill, Thomas W.; Linda C. Meyer; and Arthur M. Fischman
1979 The Aftermath of Rape. Lexington: Lexington Books.

Purpose: To present results of the first large scale, comprehensive study of the victims of rape.
Method: Detailed interviews were conducted with 1,401 women who reported a rape or sexual assault to the police in Philadelphia, 1972-1975. Court and police records were also used.
Findings: This study does not deal exclusively with acquaintance rape, but victim-offender relationship is an important variable in the results. Those findings that are most relevant for acquaintance rape are reported here. About half of the rapes were committed by an acquaintance of the victim. Women who were raped by a casual acquaintance or a relative stranger (someone the woman had seen but had not spoken to) experienced the most difficult adjustment problems. In terms of the handling of cases by the criminal justice system, the results indicate that the police were more likely to use a lesser sexual offense charge when the offender was not a stranger. Stranger rapes were less likely to be solved by the police; i.e., less likely to result in an arrest. These cases received less police investigative thoroughness than stranger cases, and they experienced more difficulty at the point of the trial due to the usual discrepancy between the story of the victim and the story presented by the defense of the offender. Offenders who were acquaintances received lighter prison terms or no prison

terms. In sum, there were effects of victim-offender relationship on the consequences of the rape for the victim and on the treatment of the case by the system. Later work on the consequences of acquaintance rape has built on this impressive beginning.

3.11 McKinney, Kathleen
1986 "Measures of Verbal, Physical, and Sexual Dating Violence By Gender." Free Inquiry in Creative Sociology 14,1:55-60.

Purpose: To review the literature on courtship violence, to examine courtship violence on a large university campus, and to provide a comparison of measures of courtship violence.
Method: 163 students (78 men and 85 women) at Oklahoma State University formed the convenience sample used in the study. Each student completed a self-administered questionnaire which collected data about background information, frequency of verbal, sexual, and physical abuse in family of origin, personal definitions of courtship violence, and involvement in dating abuse. A two part measure was developed to assess dating abuse. In this abstract, only the findings on sexual abuse are be reported.
Findings: 26% of the women and seven percent of the men reported being victims of sexual courtship violence. Men (4%) were more likely to report being sexually abusive than women (2%). There is a statistically significant relationship between experiencing abuse in one's family of origin and being a victim or perpetrator of sexual courtship abuse. The relationship, however, was weak. This may be a result of limited modeling of force sexual behavior and intercourse within families of origin. A comparison of measures of courtship violence is provided.

3.12 Muehlenhard, Charlene L. and Melaney A. Linton
1987 "Date Rape and Sexual Aggression in Dating Situations: Incidence and Risk Factors." Journal of Counseling Psychology 34,2:186-196.

Purpose: The objectives of this research were to assess the incidence of, and to determine risk factors for, male sexual aggression towards a dating partner.
Method: Questionnaires were administered to 635 male and female undergraduates. The instruments included items regarding the subject's most recent date, and regarding the worst date involving sexual aggression, if any. They also included a list of 17 sexual behaviors, for which subjects were instructed to rate which behaviors were willingly engaged in, which ones the man attempted to force on the woman, and which ones he succeeded in forcing on the woman, for each of the two dates. Subjects were then asked to complete four scales: the Attitudes Toward Women Scale; the Adversarial Sexual Beliefs Scale; the Acceptance of Interpersonal Violence Scale; and the Rape Myth Acceptance Scale.
Findings: Sexual aggression (SA) was reported by 77.6% of the females and 57.3% of the males. 14.7% of the females and 7.1% of the males reported involvement in forced sexual intercourse. Experiencing SA did not appear to be related to subjects' typical dating behavior. The SA dates were more likely than recent dates to have been initiated by the man, to have involved no expenses, to have involved heavy usage of alcohol by both persons, and to have consisted of parking somewhere in a car driven by the man. If expenses were incurred on SA dates, they were more likely to have been paid by the man. Both sexes reported that the man felt more led on, and that both persons were more suggestively dressed, on the SA dates. Males scored higher than females on all of the attitudinal scales, and subjects who had been involved in SA scored higher than those who had not.

3.13 Ploughman, Penelope and John Stensrud
1986 "The Ecology of Rape Victimization: A Case Study of Buffalo, New York." Genetic, Social, and General Psychology Monographs 112,3:303-324.

Purpose: This research used an ecological, routine activities framework to identify risk factors for rape.
Method: The authors examined data from all rapes reported to Buffalo, NY police in 1975 (n=263). Victimization triangles were used to analyze the spatial relationship between the location of the assault and other locations such as the residences of victim and perpetrator.
Findings: Young (15-24 years old), non-white, and single women were found to be at the greatest risk for rape victimization, as were highly mobile women (especially students). Rapes were more likely to be intraracial and to be committed by strangers. Initial encounters were most likely to occur on the street, although a substantial number of rapes were completed inside residences. Offenders were most likely to be nonwhite, and between the ages of 15 and 34. Victimization in particular locations was correlated with the amount of time spent in that location. Regarding the victimization triangles, a woman was most likely to be victimized in the offender's neighborhood, followed by her own neighborhood. Stranger rapes were more likely to be committed in impersonal locations such as the street, while acquaintance rapes were more likely to be committed in a personal location such as the residence of one of the parties. The findings support the use of an ecological, routine activities approach to understanding crime victimizations such as rape. this study differentiates between stranger and acquaintance rape, although it does not deal with acquaintance rape extensively. The reliance on police data explains the finding of greater likelihood of stranger rape.

3.14 Richardson, Deborah R. and Georgina S. Hammock
1991 "Alcohol and Acquaintance Rape." Pp. 83-95 in Acquaintance Rape: The Hidden Crime, edited by Andrea Parrot and Laurie Bechhofer. New York: John Wiley and Sons.

Purpose: To examine the role of alcohol in acquaintance rape.
Method: Review of literature.
Findings: The limited research on the use of alcohol by the perpetrator or victim of acquaintance rape suggests a link, but methodological weaknesses in the research prevent conclusions about whether alcohol actually increases the probability of acquaintance rape. Experimental studies that manipulate the consumption of alcohol show that alcohol may facilitate aggressive behavior and may be used as an excuse for unacceptable behavior. The research reviewed cannot be used to confirm that alcohol causes rape; rather, "alcohol affects victims and perpetrators in a variety of ways that may enhance the probability that a rape will occur."

3.15 Rouse, Linda P.; Richard Breen; and Marilyn Howell
1988 "Abuse in Intimate Relationships: A Comparison of Married and Dating College Students." Journal of Interpersonal Violence 3,4:414-429.

Purpose: To compare incidence of abuse in married and dating college relationships, examine the effects of sexual intimacy and duration on levels of abuse on intimate abuse, and consider theoretical implications.
Method: A questionnaire was distributed and completed by a convenience sample of undergraduate students at a southwestern university. A sample of 130 married undergraduates and a randomly selected subsample of 130 heterosexual, dating undergraduates were used in the study. Abuse was measured using the Stacey and Shupe scale including questions about possessiveness, sexual abuse, and physical force in intimate relationships. Only the analysis concerning sexual abuse is

discussed in this abstract. Information was also gathered concerning length of relationship and degree of sexual involvement (dating partners only).
Findings: Men and women in dating relationships did not different significantly in reports of feeling pressured by partner to have sex. However, men reported feeling more pressured than women. In married relationships, women reported feeling more pressured than men. There appears to be a relationship between sexual intimacy and dating abuse. Of those dating relationships involving intercourse, 29 percent did not report sexual pressure compared to 48 percent of the dating couples that were not sexually active. No relationship was found between length of relationship and sexual pressure for either married or dating couples.

3.16 Russell, Diana E. H.
1974 The Politics of Rape: The Victim's Perspective. New York: Stein and Day.

Purpose: The author's goal was provide accounts of rape, from the victim's perspective, in order to dispel common rape myths, to challenge unsympathetic opinions, and to highlight the many different types of circumstances under which rapes can and do take place.
Method: 90 women were interviewed about their personal experiences with rape.
Findings: The feelings of rape victims are explored. The commission of rape is linked with other social problems, such as gender inequality, male anger, racial tension, and violence in general.

3.17 Sarrel, Philip M. and William H. Masters
1982 "Sexual Molestation of Men by Women." Archives of Sexual Behavior 11,2:117-131.

Purpose: To demonstrate that male sex-response can result in situations of sexual molestation. Post-Trauma reactions to

molestation are examined. The intention is to increase identification of male victims and improve services to them. This study is primarily descriptive. Its relevance to acquaintance rape may only be the awareness of possible male victims.
Method: 11 males were interviewed by the authors. Abuse was categorized as forced assault, "baby-sitter" abuse (young man or boy seduced by an older woman or other female, with implied threats for telling), incestuous abuse (by a female relative), and "dominant woman" abuse (aggressive approach that intimidates without force). Each subject is reported as a brief case study.
Findings: Excepting two cases, all described their experience negatively. Post-traumatic impact was seen in many areas of sexual functioning. As a result of functioning where a "normal" man would not, they regarded their behavior as abnormal, which showed itself in feelings of inadequacy. Several psychophysiological explanations were put forth. They noted similarities in sexual response and its disturbing effects between men and women. That part of the post-traumatic experience is tied to the victims self-attributions concerning their physical response has definite policy implications for both health and counseling personnel.

3.18 Schneider, D. Jean; Donald Blydenburgh; and Gail Craft
1981 "Some Factors for Analysis in Sexual Assault." Social Science and Medicine 15A:55-61.

Purpose: To examine the effects of race and ethnicity, age, time of day, use of weapons, location, and relationship between victim and perpetrator on rape.
Method: A questionnaire was used to collect data about the victims and perpetrators of 248 reported sexual assault cases. Information was gathered concerning age, sex, ethnicity, type of location, day and time of assault, armed status of perpetrator, and relationship between perpetrator and victim.
Findings: In fifty-nine percent of the assaults, the victim and the perpetrator knew each other. Fifty-five percent of the multi-assailant cases involved acquaintances. A wide variety of

relationships were found. Considering the characteristics of acquaintance sexual assaults, victims tend to be younger than their perpetrators, the assaults tend to occur on weekend nights, in the victim's home, and they tend not to involve the use of weapons.

3.19 Struckman-Johnson, Cindy
1991 "Male Victims of Acquaintance Rape." Pp 192-214 in Acquaintance Rape: The Hidden Crime, edited by Andrea Parrot and Laurie Bechhofer. New York: John Wiley and Sons.

Purpose: To review the research on male victims of acquaintance rape. There is very little research on male victims, so this chapter raises many questions for future research.
Method: Review of literature.
Findings: There is a lack of research on male victims, but the few community and college campus surveys that provide any data indicate that a substantial minority of men have been sexually assaulted. Many of these assaults are perpetrated by men, and the dynamics of male rape by men are similar to those of female rape by men. There are also documented cases of men being pressured or forced to have unwanted sexual contact with a female. The scanty evidence that exists suggests that men can be seriously harmed by these female assaults. More research is needed on the consequences of sexual assault of men by women and the motivation of the sexually coercive female. Recommendations include more education about the existence of male victims and improved treatment programs for the victims. And, of course, more research is needed, since very little has been done to date.

4

MISPERCEPTIONS OF SEXUAL INTENT

4.1 Abbey, Antonia
1982 "Sex Differences in Attributions for Friendly Behavior: Do Males Misperceive Females' Friendliness?" Journal of Personality and Social Psychology 42,5:830-838.

Purpose: The study tests the hypothesis that friendliness from a member of the opposite sex might be perceived as a sign of sexual interest.
Method: Male and female undergraduate students participated in a lab experiment that involved an interaction between a man and a woman. Participants viewed the interaction and were asked to attribute the actors' behavior as flirtatious, promiscuous, and seductive. They were also asked if they would like to get to know the actors, if they were sexually attracted to the opposite sex actor, and if they wanted to date him or her.
Findings: Men rated the female actor as significantly more promiscuous and thought that she wanted to be friends with, was sexually attracted to, and wanted to date the male actor. Men also indicated that they were more sexually attracted to and wanted to date the opposite sex actor than women did.

4.2 Abbey, Antonia
1987 "Misperceptions of Friendly Behavior as Sexual

Interest: A Survey of Naturally Occurring Incidents." Psychology of Women Quarterly 11, 173-194.

Purpose: The study examines the differences between the genders as well as attributions assigned to misperception.
Method: Two undergraduate populations responded to a survey that examined their experience with having their friendly behavior misperceived as sexual by a member of the opposite sex.
Findings: The data indicate that both men's and women's friendly behavior is misinterpreted as sexual, but the situations in which they are misperceived vary by gender. Women were more likely to be misperceived in a party situation, whereas men's experiences often happened in public places such as classrooms or the student union. When their behavior is misperceived, men were more likely to ignore the misperception and women were more likely to ask the misperceiver to stop their behavior. In assigning attributions, women were more likely to assign external causes, such as alcohol, to the misperceived behavior, while men were more likely to assign internal causes, such as the person's personality. Overall, alcohol consumption, the person's clothing, and flirtation were also rated as moderately likely causes of misperception. Prior sexual activity, misperceiver's reputation, and adversarial male/female relations were seen as unlikely causes of misperception.

4.3 Abbey, Antonia
1991 "Misperception as an Antecedent of Acquaintance Rape: A Consequence of Ambiguity in Communication Between Women and Men." Pp. 96-112 in Acquaintance Rape: The Hidden Crime, edited by Andrea Parrot and Laurie Bechhofer. New York: John Wiley and Sons.

Purpose: To review the research on misperceptions of sexual intent.
Method: Review of literature.
Findings: The research on misperception of sexual intent shows

that misperceptions of sexual intent are very common in American society and that men are more likely than women to misperceive friendly behavior as indicative of sexual interest. Ambiguous cues, such as nonverbal cues, clothing, and drug or alcohol use, enhance the likelihood for misperceptions. Most of the research on misperceptions has relied on samples of white, middle-class college students; far less is known about misperceptions among other groups. The research that has been done indicates that misperceptions frequently contribute to acquaintance rape. Educational programs need to emphasize the importance of direct communication about sexual intents and desires.

4.4 Abbey, Antonia; Catherine Cozzarelli; Kimberly McLaughlin; and Richard J. Harnish
1987 "The Effects of Clothing and Dyad Sex Composition on Perceptions of Sexual Intent: Do Women and Men Evaluate These Cues Differently?" Journal of Applied Social Psychology 17,2:108-126

Purpose: Abbey (1982) demonstrated that, compared to women, men tend to rate both males and females as more seductive and promiscuous. Regarding this, what will be the effect of clothing ("revealing" vs. "nonrevealing") and dyad composition on the subjects' interpretation of sexual intent and perception of sexual traits? This is the question they address.
Method: Subjects were 287 university undergraduates (12 subjects were assigned to each condition, except one which received 11). Each subject examined three photographs, two fillers and one stimulus, and filled out a questionnaire for each one. The subjects evaluated the persons in the photograph on a Likert-type scale, for traits such as seductiveness, sexy, promiscuous; but also the traits friendly, cheerful, kind, etc.
Findings: As per hypotheses, males did tend to rate female targets higher on sexual traits than females did. This held for female/female dyads as well as male/female dyads. The predicted interaction between dyad composition and clothing revealingness was not seen. Both males and females rated female targets as

more flirtatious, sexy, seductive, and promiscuous when they wore revealing outfits. The revealingness of male target clothing did not increase subjects' perceptions of their sexual traits. The was little to support the prediction that men perceived male targets higher on sexual traits than females did. Both male and female targets in nonrevealing outfits were described as more likeable, warmer, and friendlier than their counterparts.

4.5 Abbey, Antonia and Christian Melby
1986 "The Effects of Nonverbal Cues on Gender Differences in Perceptions of Sexual Intent." Sex Roles 15:283-298.

Purpose: To examine the interpretation of sexual intent by males and females of non-verbal signaling (touch, eye-contact, distance). It was hypothesized that men would make greater attributions of sexuality to a greater extent than women.
Method: Subjects were 246 university undergraduates. Each subject was randomly assigned to one of ten nonverbal cue scenarios (3 distance, 2 eye-contact, 5 touch). Subjects examined photographs, two "fillers" and one actual stimulus, then filled out a questionnaire for each one. The target photograph depicted a young couple sitting at a table with varying degrees of the nonverbal cues present. For the target photo only, respondents were asked to answer questions regarding romantic involvement between the couple pictured, and their sexual attractiveness to each other.
Findings: Males rated the female target higher on sexual traits than females did in all scenarios. She was also seen as more promiscuous by males than by females in eye contact scenarios. Males were more sexually attracted to the opposite sexed target than females were. Sexual-trait ratings were not influenced by ambiguous cuing. At closer distances, the targets received higher ratings of friendship and romantic involvement. Subjects did not rate targets who make eye contact as more likely to be romantically linked. Overall, men tended to view the female with a higher degree of sexuality than women did.

4.6 LaPlante, Marcia; Naomi McCormick; and Gary Brannigan
1980 "Living the Sexual Script: College Student's Views of Influence in Sexual Encounters." Journal of Sex Research 16,4:338-355.

Purpose: To study the relationships among gender, local of control, stereotypes about sexual influence, and personal experiences in sexual encounters.
Method: One hundred and twenty four undergraduate students participated in a study about dating attitudes. Students were asked to indicate their extent of heterosexual erotic experience and sexual preference. Additionally, subjects responded to two questionnaires. The first was the Rotter Locus of Control Scale. The other was the Sexual Script Questionnaire, which contains two examples each of ten strategies for having sexual intercourse and nine strategies for avoiding sexual intercourse. Subjects were asked to categorize these responses based on gender and to indicate how often they used similar strategies.
Findings: Subjects indicated that they practice and prescribe sexual scripts that involve men using a variety of strategies to obtain sexual intercourse and women employing strategies to avoid sexual intercourse. There were significant differences between strategies used to have/avoid sexual intercourse and locus of control. Despite the fact that society has become more sexually liberated, this study supports the notion that traditional sexual scripts are still widely accepted and practiced. This study does not deal specifically with acquaintance rape. However, the study is relevant to acquaintance rape in the emphasis on college student sexual scripts, which are related to sexual misperceptions.

4.7 Shotland, R. Lance and Jane M. Craig
1988 "Can Men and Women Differentiate between Friendly and Sexually Interested Behavior?" Social Psychology Quarterly 51:66-73.

Purpose: To examine gender differences in attribution of sexual intent and differentiation between "sexually interested" and

"friendly" actions.
Method: For the experiment used in this study, a sample of 81 male and 85 female undergraduate students were randomly assigned to two groups. Subjects watched a videotape of mixed-gender groups and were then asked to describe the men and women in the video, the sexual attraction between the men and women (measured with the sexual interest scale, SIS), and the couple's relationship (global sexual interest scale).
Findings: Men were more likely than women to perceive the men and women in the video to be sexually interested in their partners. However, both men and women were able to differentiate between sexually interested and friendly behavior. Thus, it is concluded that men are able to interpret the behavioral cues of women, even when cues may appear to be ambiguous. Still, men were more likely than women to perceive situations as sexually oriented. This is believed to be a result of different thresholds of sexual interest.

4.8 Sigal, Janet; Margaret Gibbs; Bonnie Adams; and Richard Derfler
1988 "The Effect of Romantic and Nonromantic Films on Perception of Female Friendly and Seductive Behavior." Sex Roles 19,9/10:545-554.

Purpose: To examine the extent of gender differences in the perception of behaviors objectively defined as "friendly" and "seductive." Also, to examine whether the viewing of romantic films would enhance the subject's sexually oriented interpretations of both friendly and seductive cues.
Method: Two experiments were used. In the first, 57 male and 56 female introductory psychology students were randomly assigned to view videotapes of scenes varied by gender of (main) actor, and whether they were "friendly" or "seductive." After viewing, subjects completed 25 7-point semantic differential scales, which were used to form three scales. All subjects then completed the Spence-Helmreich PAQ. In the second experiment, the procedure outlined above was repeated after the subjects viewed either a romantic or nonromantic film clip.

Findings: In the first experiment, both male and female subjects rated the actor in the "seductive" scene as the more seductive. No gender difference hypotheses were confirmed. In the second experiment, the "priming" effect of viewing the romantic film was not observed. However, males were more likely to view the female actor as being seductive regardless of which film was viewed. Subjects who viewed the nonromantic film prior to the "seductive" videotape were more likely to rate the female actor as being flirtatious than those who viewed the "friendly" videotape. Subjects who viewed the romantic film before viewing the seductive video were less likely to rate the female actor as promiscuous. Male sexual misinterpretation increased as the cues became more subtle.

4.9 Warshaw, Robin and Andrea Parrot
1991 "The Contribution of Sex-Role Socialization to Acquaintance Rape." Pp. 73-82 in Acquaintance Rape: The Hidden Crime, edited by Andrea Parrot and Laurie Bechhofer. New York: John Wiley and Sons.

Purpose: To review the literature on the effects of sex-role socialization on acquaintance rape.
Method: Review of literature.
Findings: Sex-role socialization is pervasive, and messages about appropriate sex roles are found in family patterns, in the media, in schools, and in peer groups. Men are socialized to believe their sex drives are uncontrollable, and that women do not mean "no" when they say "no." Women are socialized to believe that "nice" men do not rape and that if she is victimized, she is to blame. The result is that men and women have different orientations to sexuality and this contributes to acquaintance rape.

5

RESEARCH ON PERPETRATORS

5.1 Barbaree, H.E.; W.L. Marshall; and E. Yates.
1983 "Alcohol Intoxication and Deviant Sexual Arousal in Male Social Drinkers." Behavior Research and Therapy 21,4:365-373.

Purpose: The study measures sexual arousal of men under the influence of alcohol to mutually consenting rape cues.
Method: Thirty-three male graduate students participated in a laboratory experiment which measured their sexual arousal to verbal descriptions of two sexual episodes. One depicted a mutual consent relationship between a man and woman and the other depicted a rape scene. The study also measured the effects of alcohol on sexual arousal. One group of subjects drank a beverage containing .63 ml of absolute ethanol/kg of body weight and one group drank a placebo drink.
Findings: The data indicate that subjects who drank alcohol were less likely to distinguish between sexual cues than those who did not drink alcohol. However, the description of the rape scenario evoked less sexual arousal for both groups than the mutually consenting scenario. This finding is inconsistent with previous studies that have found that alcohol increases sexual arousal levels.

5.2 Beneke, Timothy
1982 Men on Rape: What They Have to Say About

Sexual Violence. New York: St. Martin's Press.

Purpose: The author explores men's attitudes about rape through analysis of the language and other symbols men use in conceptualizing women and sexuality.
Method: The research consisted of interviews with "normal men," rapists, husbands and lovers, police, doctors and lawyers.
Findings: The idea that rape is a manifestation of men's anger is revealed. From this perspective, rape is viewed as one point on a continuum of violence against women. Although, as the author admits, this research is less than scientific, it is nonetheless quite useful for sensitizing the reader to the kinds of "acceptable" sexual attitudes and expressions which ultimately serve as justifications for sexual violence against women.

5.3 Briere, John and Neil M. Malamuth
1983 "Self-Reported Likelihood of Sexually Aggressive Behavior: Attitudinal Versus Sexual Explanations." Journal of Research in Personality 17:315-323.

Purpose: This study presents a comparative analysis of two perspectives on the causes of rape, using a sexual explanation and a social/attitudinal explanation. The first sees a proclivity toward sexual violence as caused by sexual frustration or maladjustment, the second, as being caused by a variety of rape supportive beliefs and attitudes.
Method: The subjects were 352 male undergraduates. They were presented with a "Sexual Attitudes Survey," containing items for the self-reported likelihood of rape, use of sexual force, and scales for the disbelief of rape claims. It also included items to form a sexuality scale. Subjects were then classified as 1) no likelihood of rape, 2) no likelihood of force but some likelihood to rape, 3) some likelihood of force but no likelihood of rape, and 4) some likelihood of both force and rape.
Findings: 28% of the subjects reported some likelihood of both rape and force, 2% indicated some likelihood of rape but not

force, 30% reported some likelihood of force but not rape, and 40% reported no likelihood of force or rape. Due to the small size of the likelihood to rape but not use force (n=6), and the counterintuitive nature of the concept, those falling into this category were excluded from the analysis. Membership in each of the three remaining categories was predicted on the basis of rape-supportive beliefs. Sexuality variables could not discriminate between these groups. Males in the "force but not rape" and the "force and rape" groups had higher scores in victim responsibility, male dominance, adversarial sexual beliefs, and rape reports as manipulation scales. The sexual experience variable was the only sexual variable to have any predictive power. The authors suggest that we may need to look more toward changes in values and attitudes rather than treatment of "sexual psychopaths."

5.4 Greendlinger, Virginia and Donn Byrne
1987 "Coercive Sexual Fantasies of College Men as Predictors of Self-Reported Likelihood to Rape and Overt Sexual Aggression." Journal of Sex Research 23, 1:1-11.

Purpose: The study explores the relationship of men's coercive sexual fantasies, their hypothetical willingness to rape, and self reports of past sexual aggression.
Method: One hundred and fourteen undergraduate men responded to the Rape Myth Acceptance Scale which asks subjects to rate their frequency of various sexual fantasies, preferences, and beliefs. The subjects also indicated whether they would rape a woman if they were guaranteed not to get punished for the assault. They were also asked to write a brief sexual fantasy involving force or rape. Sixty-three of the men also filled out the Sexual Experiences Survey and the Aggression Scale of the Jackson Personality Research Form.
Findings: Rape myth acceptance, aggressive tendencies, and scores on the Coercive Sexual Fantasies Scale were all significantly correlated with the likelihood of rape. Rape likelihood and rape myth acceptance seem not to be related to

actual coercive sexual behavior. Slightly over 7% of the sample indicted that they had used physical force to obtain sexual contact and 1.6% indicated that they had raped a woman. However, men also employed a variety of other tactics to obtain sex against a woman's will: 41.7% said thing they didn't mean; 13.4% pressured by continual arguments; 23% became so excited they couldn't stop themselves; and 6.7% threatened to end the relationship. An interesting finding was that less than 20% of the men agreed to write a coercive sexual fantasy. Thirty-two percent of those men who did indicated some likelihood of raping under the conditions stated.

5.5 Heilbrun, Alfred B. and Maura P. Loftus
1986 "The Role of Sadism and Peer Pressure in the Sexual Aggression of Male College Students." Journal of Sex Research 22,3:320-332.

Purpose: The study uses socialization and sadistic models to explain sexual aggression in college men.
Method: Undergraduate men responded to a dating questionnaire that included such things as the amount of time a dating couple spends together, degree of sexual intimacy, and degree of communication between the couple. Two questions related to the subject's personal experiences with sexual aggression. Subjects were then shown a series of slides representing 6 female models expressing 6 different emotions through facial expression. Subjects were asked to rate their sexual attractiveness to the women in the slides.
Findings: The data indicate that the sadistic model provides more of an explanation for sexual aggression in men. Subjects who rated the distressed faces as sexually attractive were more likely to have had a history of sexual aggression in their dating relationships. Peer pressure was not found to significantly affect sexual aggression. Of the sexually aggressive subjects, only 37% reported peer pressure for greater sexual intimacy, whereas 63% of the non-aggressive subjects indicated peer pressure. Additionally, fewer sexually aggressive men reported peer pressure

to take sexual advantage of women than was true for the sexually non-aggressive men.

5.6 Kanin, Eugene J.
1965 "Male Sex Aggression and Three Psychiatric Hypotheses." Journal of Sex Research 1:221-231.

Purpose: To test three psychiatric hypotheses by examining the effects of general hostility towards women, sex drive, and general aggressiveness on male sexual aggression.
Method: The questionnaire was distributed and completed by a sample of 341 undergraduate university males. Sexually aggressive acts were defined by self reports of forceful attempts for coitus which were disagreeable or offensive to the woman, perceptions of female offended reactions, and description of the act. Hostility towards women was measured as the quality of the mother-son relationship (7-point scale), negative experiences with women and interpersonal relationships, and a lack of female siblings. Sex drive was measured as an estimation of the number of ejaculations required per week for sexual satisfaction. General aggressiveness was measured using the Zaks and Walters scale.
Findings: General hostility towards women. The aggressive and the nonaggressive men differed significantly in the love for their mothers; thus, there is support for the hypothesis that sexually aggressive men tend to have negative feelings towards their mothers. Aggressive men were also much more likely than nonaggressive men to have experienced acts of deception, infidelity, and unexplained termination in an interpersonal relationship with a woman. No significant difference was found between aggressive and nonaggressive men in the presence of female siblings. Sex drive. Aggressive and nonaggressive men differed significantly on the number of ejaculations estimated for satisfaction; aggressive men have higher subjective estimates of their sex drive than nonaggressive men. General aggressiveness. The sexually aggressive men were significantly more aggressive in general than sexually nonaggressive men. Sexual aggression

appears to be strongly correlated with aggressive behavior in general.

This is a good example of a work that led, among others, to the eventual conceptualization of the category of "date rape," but not one that uses that category. The study predates the conceptualization of a separate and identifiable phenomenon of "date" or "acquaintance" rape.

5.7 Kanin, Eugene J.
1967 "An Examination of Sexual Aggression as a Response to Sexual Frustration." Journal of Marriage and the Family 29:428-433.

Purpose: To test the popular belief that male sexual aggression in the context of dating activity is a result of frustration caused by an unavailability of consensual heterosexual outlets.
Method: Data were collected through interviews with 341 fulltime, undergraduate males randomly selected from a midwestern university. The sexual histories of sexually aggressive and nonaggressive men were compared. Sexually aggressive behavior was measured by asking about perceptions of disagreement and offended reactions by female partners and descriptions of aggressive acts.
Findings: Aggressive males were significantly more sexually active than nonaggressive males. They were more involved in non-physically aggressive sexual intercourse and coitus or genital petting. Aggressive males showed a significantly stronger desire to gain new sexual experience, report more sexually exploitative behavior in high school and college, and utilized more sexual exploitation techniques than nonaggressive males, such as attempting to intoxicate their partner, falsely professing love, and threatening to terminate the relationship. In addition, aggressive males, although experiencing more sexual activity, reported significantly more dissatisfaction with their sexual activities over the past year than nonaggressive males. Thus, sexual satisfaction is not necessarily determined by the amount of sexual activity.

Other findings show that over 82% of aggressive males reported peer pressure for new sexual experiences compared to 58% percent of the nonaggressive males. Therefore, sexual satisfaction needs to be considered within the context of sexual aspirations. In an environment where sexual experience is encouraged and pressured by peers and as a result, sexual aspirations are high, relative deprivation is likely. Thus, male desires for sexual outlets appear to be the result of frustration created by peer group association.

5.8 Kanin, Eugene J.
1967 "Reference Groups and Sex Conduct Norm Violations." Sociological Quarterly 8:495-504.

Purpose: To examine the relationship between peer reference groups and the norm violation of male sexual aggression in dating relationships. Specifically, the aim of the study is to test the hypothesis that aggressive males are members of peer reference groups that not only sanction but encourage sexual experience.
Method: 341 fulltime, undergraduate males randomly selected from a midwestern university were interviewed. Sexually aggressive behavior was measured by asking about their perceptions of disagreement and offended reactions by female partners and descriptions of aggressive acts.
Findings: Aggressive males reported a significantly greater degree of pressure by friends for new sexual experience than nonaggressive males. Furthermore, 49.4% of aggressive males as compared to 28.3% of nonaggressive males believed that admitting virginity would result in a loss of status. Thus, aggressive males appear to have a greater association with peers who value and encourage sexual experience. Actual sexual experience reflects these values in that only 32.7% of the aggressive males but 62.1% of the non-aggressive males were virgins. However, aggressive males were significantly less satisfied than nonaggressive males with their sexual activities of the past year. This is likely to be a result of the relative deprivation that occurs from high aspirations associated with being a member of a group that emphasizes and

values sexual experience. Aggressive males tend to be significantly more likely to be members of one such reference group, college social fraternities. Results also show that sexually aggressive behavior is not necessarily a recent result of peer group association in college. Instead, the aggressive men were significantly more sexually aggressive in high school as well. Aggressive males tend to seek out the peer groups that support and sustain their behavior and values. Finally findings show that peer reference groups that encourage and value sexual experience work to justify sexually aggressive behavior which violates norms. Justification learned from peers is usually based on the perceived behavior of the woman labeling her a "teaser," "golddigger," or "loose." The more pressure for sex experience males receive, the more sexual aggression is justified.

5.9 Kanin, Eugene J.
1971 "Sexually Aggressive College Males." The Journal of College Student Personnel 12:107-110.

Purpose: To draw attention to male sex aggression, the use of physical force to obtain sex from an unwilling female partner, on college campuses. The study includes a discussion of incidence and frequency of sexual aggression, female reactions to sexual aggression, characteristics of pair relationships, erotic histories of aggressive males, hostility towards women, general aggressive behavior, and adjustive reactions.
Method: Integrative review of previously published and unpublished findings from three different studies at two large, midwestern universities.
Findings: Incidence and prevalence. Approximately one-fourth of a random sample of male college students reported sexually aggressive behavior since entering college. The mean number of reported sexually aggressive acts was 2.1. Female reactions to sexual aggression. Few women relied on the assistance of institutional authorities after experiencing acts of sexual aggression because of the associated need to report level of voluntary sexual activity and shared stigma. The relationship to the male aggressor

is more influential than severity of aggression in determining reactions to sexual aggression. Women in early dating relationships respond with first reactions and violence. Women in more established relationships are most likely to cry showing disillusionment. Pair relationships. Sexual aggression tends to occur significantly more when offender and victim are heterogeneous in terms of religion, age, social status, and intelligence. Erotic history of sexually aggressive males. Erotic histories can be characterized as predatory. Sexually aggressive behavior occurred since high school and involves a variety of tactics of aggression. The males continually strive for sexual activity. Although usually sexually active, they view themselves as sexually deprived as a result of high sexual aspirations and relative deprivation based on peer references group values. Hostility towards women. Aggressive males had difficulty in mother-son and heterosexual relationships which result in negative assessment of women. General aggressiveness. Sexual aggression tends to be part of more general aggressive behavior. Adjustive reactions. Approximately half of aggressive males reported that they did not justify their behavior. Those men that did justify their behavior generally have peers that value and encourage sexual activity and place the responsibility for the aggressive behavior on the woman. Such justification is associated with the male's social class and religiosity.

5.10 Kanin, Eugene J.
1984 "Date Rape: Unofficial Criminals and Victims." Victimology 9,1:95-108.

Purpose: The study investigates the personal and social characteristics of self-disclosed date rapists.
Method: During a 10 year period, 71 male undergraduate students voluntarily presented themselves to the researcher as possible rapists willing to be interviewed and respond to a questionnaire.
Findings: All of the men had prior consensual relations with the woman that they assaulted. Two factors were identified to explain

their rape behavior. The first deals with the rapist's perception that the victim was sexually aroused, which in turn aroused them. They indicate that their own arousal was so strong that they ignored attempts by the woman to stop the behavior. Alcohol accounts for the second motivating factor. Two thirds of the population indicated that excessive drinking as a causal factor for the assault. The author suggests that there is a sexual dimension to date rape and that theories of power or violence are not the only factors operating in these situations.

5.11 Kanin, Eugene J.
1985 "Date Rapists: Differential Sexual Socialization and Relative Deprivation." Archives of Sexual Behavior 14,3:219-231.

Purpose: The study examines variables that are responsible for men raping.
Method: Seventy-one undergraduate male students volunteered over a ten year period to participate in an interview and respond to a questionnaire. All of the men were self-disclosed date rapists. This group was compared to a control group of 227 undergraduate males.
Findings: The date rapists indicated that they had more sexual encounters, more successful sexual encounters than the control group, and require more orgasms per week to satisfy their sexual desires. They were also more likely to employ coercive techniques to obtain sex from females. Peer pressure played an important role in date rapists sexual encounters in both college and high school. One of the most striking differences between the two groups had to do with justifiability of rape, with 86% of date rapists, compared to 19% of the control group, indicating rape was justified under certain conditions.

5.12 Koss, Mary P. and Thomas E. Dinero.
1988 "Predictors of Sexual Aggression among a National Sample of Male College Students." Pp.

113-146 in Human Sexual Aggression: Current Perspectives, edited by Robert A. Prentky and Vernon L. Quinsey. New York: Annals of the New York Academy of Sciences.

Purpose: To explore the potential for sexual aggression in a nonclinical sample of men.
Method: 2,972 males from a random national sample of 6,159 undergraduates completed a questionnaire including the following: the Sexual Experiences Survey; items relevant to Finkelhor's preconditions and releasers of sexually abusive behavior; the Hostility Toward Women Scale; the short-form of the MMPI Psychopathic Deviate Scale; the Rape Supportive Beliefs Scale; the Extended Personal Attributes Scale; and questions about current behavior, including use of alcohol and pornography, the Conflict Tactics Scale, and peer relations.
Findings: 600 of the men in the sample reported committing some form of sexual aggression since the age of 14, 131 of which met the legal definition of rape. Subjects' childhood experiences, psychological characteristics, and current behavior were predictive of 5 increasing levels of sexual aggression. Early and more childhood sexual activity (both forced and voluntary), hostility towards women, belief in the legitimacy of force as a way to obtain sexual contact, use of alcohol and violent/degrading pornography, and involvement with peers who share a highly sexualized view of women were all associated with reports of more severe sexual aggression. Sexual aggression does not necessarily occur on a simple continuum of behavior.

5.13 Koss, Mary; Kenneth Leonard; Dana Beezley; and Cheryl Oros

1985 "Nonstranger Sexual Aggression: A Discriminant Analysis of the Psychological Characteristics of Undetected Offenders." Sex Roles 12,9/10:981-993.

Purpose: The study examines the psychological characteristics of three types of undetected sexually aggressive men who had assaulted female acquaintances.

Method: Men involved in this study were chosen based on their responses to the Sexual Experiences Survey. Subjects were classified into four groups to determine their level of sexual aggression: sexually assaultive, sexually abusive, sexually coercive, and sexually nonaggressive. The men participated in an indepth interview that examined their psychopathic tendencies, acceptance of traditional sex role stereotypes, and rape supportive beliefs.

Findings: Men who have threatened to or actually used force to gain nonconsensual intercourse adhered to several rape supportive attitudes. They were more likely to attribute adversarial qualities to interpersonal relationships, accept sex role stereotypes, believe myths about rape, feel that rape prevention is women's responsibility, and view sex and aggression as going together. The social control/conflict model of rape suggests that accepted customs in society foster as well as encourage men to rape. The data from this study indicate the importance of rape myths in discriminating men who engage in sexual aggression and those who don't. On the other hand, the psychopathology model suggests that rape is a result of the person's personality characteristics. The men in this study could not be distinguished from one another based on their personality characteristics. The authors suggest that the social control model should be applied to studying self identified acquaintance rapist and the psychopathology model may be more appropriate for incarcerated populations.

5.14 Mahoney, E.R.; Michael D. Shively; and Marsha Traw
1986 "Sexual Coercion and Assault: Male Socialization and Female Risk." Sexual Coercion and Assault 1,1:2-8.

Purpose: To identify male socialization traits associated with rape and sexual assault, and to examine correlates of female experience with sexual assault. Is female experience random, or are there

predispositional characteristics?
Method: Subjects were 130 male and 207 female undergraduates. They completed a survey containing scales for coercive sexuality, macho personality (or attraction to macho men), attitudes towards women, locus of control, and sexuality.
Findings: For males, sexual coercion was correlated with macho personality, coital experience, number of lifetime partners, years of sexual activity, and number of partners per year. For females, the number (of types) of sexually coercive activities, correlated with extensiveness of sexual contact with males. These findings were interpreted as suggesting that for males sexual coercion is mainly related to the opportunity to do so. Having a macho personality increases the likelihood of this. Female victimization was seen as a function of risk in the form of exposure. Other individual characteristics such as religiosity, gender role orientation, and locus of control were not related to assault experiences.

5.15 Malamuth, Neil M.
1981 "Rape Proclivity Among Males." Journal of Social Issues 37,4:138-157.

Purpose: The author's objective was to integrate existing research in an effort to begin to formulate theory about men's rape proclivity.
Method: Research Review
Findings: Evidence suggests that many men have some propensity to rape. Identified rapists are likely to believe in rape myths, to have little remorse about raping, and to become aroused by rape depictions. Sexually aggressive men are more likely to believe that rape victims actually wanted sex. General aggression towards women is highly related to sexual aggression. Nonrapists are less aroused by rape depictions except when victim is described as being aroused. Rape proclivity is associated with a view of rape as an inconsequential event.

The author suggests several issues for further research. First, more detailed information should be obtained when asking men about their perceived propensity to commit rape. For example, subjects should be asked why they believe they are capable of committing rape. Second, more needs to be known about the consequences of self-reported rape proclivity; do such men avoid or seek out potentially aggressive sexual situations? Third, information obtained from those with high self-reported rape proclivity should be used to inform efforts to reduce tolerance for rape. Finally, more information on other characteristics of men with a propensity to rape (e.g. violence in the family of origin, attitudes towards women) needs to be collected.

5.16 Malamuth, Neil M.
1986 "Predictors of Naturalistic Sexual Aggression." Journal of Personality and Social Psychology 50:953-962.

Purpose: To examine potential predictors of male sexual aggression against women in a naturalistic setting.
Method: The study was performed in two stages. (1) 155 men completed a questionnaire to gather data concerning sexual aggressive behavior and predictors. Sexual aggression was measured using the Koss and Oros instrument. The predictors were measured as follows: Dominance as sexual motive; Hostility towards women; Attitudes facilitating violence; Antisocial characteristics; and Sexual experience. (2) A subsample of 95 men participated in an assessment of sexual arousal in response to depictions of rape and mutually consenting sex. Sexual arousal was measured using penile tumescence.
Findings: All predictors, except antisocial characteristics, were significantly related to naturalistic aggression. A combination of the predictors was found to be more predictive of sexual aggressiveness than any single predictor. The data also were more consistent with an interactive model of combining the predictors. It is concluded that the presence of only one predictor is unlikely to lead to high levels of sexual aggression. The findings suggest that there is similarity between predictors of stranger and acquaintance rape. In the general population, a substantial number

of men have arousal patterns similar to those of convicted rapists. The findings support the views that sexual arousal in response to aggression and sexually aggressive media depictions are related to sexually aggressive behavior in men.

5.17 Malamuth, Neil and Karol E. Dean
1991 "Attraction to Sexual Aggression." Pp. 229-248 in Acquaintance Rape: The Hidden Crime, edited by Andrea Parrot and Laurie Bechhofer. New York: John Wiley and Sons.

Purpose: To review research on attraction to sexual aggression, as opposed to actual sexual aggression; the development of measures of attraction to sexual aggression; the relationship between attraction and actual aggression; and to identify areas for future work.
Method: Review of literature.
Findings: Three models of sexual aggression are discussed--psychodynamic theories, sociobiological factors, and feminist theory. Each could include the addition of attraction to aggression. Attraction and actual aggression do not necessarily occur together, rather, there are four logical possibilities combining attraction and actual aggression. Malamuth's multi-item "attraction to sexual aggression" scale is described in detail. It is argued that this scale is more valid than earlier measures of likelihood to rape or force sex items. Future research is needed on the expectancies associated with sexual aggression, cross-cultural comparisons, cognitive and affective factors associated with attraction to aggression, the impact of self-awareness of such attraction, and factors that prevent attraction from becoming actual sexual aggression.

5.18 Peterson, Steven and Bettina Franzese
1987 "Correlates of College Men's Sexual Abuse of Women." Journal of College Student Personnel May:223-228.

Purpose: This study examined social-psychological and political characteristics of men who are sexually aggressive towards women.
Method: 99 male undergraduate and other students completed a questionnaire which included the Sexual Experiences Survey, Rosenberg's Self-Esteem Scale, the Srole Anomie Scale, the Spielberger State-Trait Anxiety Scale, Rotter's Internal Locus-of-Control Scale, Rosenberg's Misanthropy Index, and items regarding attitudes towards women, political involvement, political ideology, political distrust, internal political efficacy, political participation, and optimism about the economic future.
Findings: Sexual abusiveness was associated with traditional attitudes about women and about rape, greater misanthropy, less internal locus of control, lower self-esteem, and lower levels of anomie. Abusers were likely to be politically conservative, to be optimistic about the future economic picture, and to be politically active.

5.19 Rapaport, Karen and Barry R. Burkhart
1984 "Personality and Attitudinal Characteristics of Sexually Coercive College Males." Journal of Abnormal Psychology 93,2:216-221

Purpose: This study identified characteristics of sexually coercive men.
Method: Questionnaires were administered to 201 undergraduate men. Instruments consisted of the Responsibility, Socialization, and Empathy scales from the California Psychological Inventory; the Sex Role Stereotyping, Own Sex Role Satisfaction, Adversarial Sexual Beliefs, Sexual Conservatism, and Acceptance of Interpersonal Violence scales; the Attitudes Towards Women scale; an endorsement of force scale; and a scale of coercive sexuality.
Findings: Less than 40% of the sample denied any sexually coercive behavior. Responsibility and Socialization were the only personality traits which were significantly related to sexual coerciveness. All of the aggression measures (Adversarial Sexual Beliefs, Acceptance of Interpersonal Violence and endorsement of

force) were predictive of coerciveness. None of the attitude measures were significant predictors of coerciveness. The authors conclude that, while sexual coercion may be seen as generally socially acceptable, only men with certain characteristics are likely to engage in it.

5.20 Rapaport, Karen R. and C. Dale Posey
1991 "Sexually Coercive College Males." Pp 217-28 in Acquaintance Rape: The Hidden Crime, edited by Andrea Parrot and Laurie Bechhofer. New York: John Wiley and Sons.

Purpose: To review the research on sexually coercive males in the general population, which provides a contrast to the research on rapists who have come to the attention of the criminal justice system.
Method: Review of literature.
Findings: Studies of sexually coercive males rely extensively on self-report data. Such reports present problems of validity, but they are revealing nonetheless. Studies have found that a majority of males acknowledge involvement in some type of coercive sexual behavior, ranging from touching to intercourse against the woman's will. Sexually coercive males are similar to noncoercive males, which supports the idea of the "normality of rapists." However, sexually coercive males do differ in significant ways from those who are noncoercive. The coercive males are more sexually arousable; they act impulsively, irresponsibly, and aggressively; and they are more likely to have adversarial sexual beliefs and to be hostile toward women. The research suggests that a comprehensive model of sexually coercive behavior must include personality, situational, and socialization components.

5.21 Wilson, Kenneth; Rebecca Faison; and G.M. Britton
1983 "Cultural Aspects of Male Sex Aggression." Deviant Behavior 4:241-255.

Purpose: The objective of this research was to come up with explanations for men's sexual aggression towards female dates.
Method: 81 men from a random sample of 250 undergraduates completed questionnaires which asked about their own experience with being sexually aggressive. Subjects were administered the Premarital Sexual Permissiveness Scale, and a scale measuring how important subjects perceived sex to be in their relationships. Subjects were also asked about powerlessness, experience of child abuse, belief in legitimate victims, belief in a double standard, and acceptance of rape myths.
Findings: Experience with child abuse, a high value placed on sex in relationships, belief in legitimate victims, and acceptance of rape myths were all strongly correlated with self-reported sexual aggression. In a path model, child abuse, acceptance of rape myths, and belief in legitimate victims had strong direct effects on sex aggression. The authors reject the hypothesis that the purpose of sex aggression is to overcome feelings of powerlessness, and suggest that social learning theory may be a better framework for understanding rape.

6

THEORETICAL PERSPECTIVES

6.1 Bechhofer, Laurie and Andrea Parrot
1991 "What is Acquaintance Rape?" Pp. 9-25 in Acquaintance Rape: The Hidden Crime, edited by Andrea Parrot and Laurie Bechhofer. New York: John Wiley and Sons.

Purpose: To provide an overview of the definition of date and acquaintance rape, the history of the development of acquaintance rape as a conceptually distinct type of sexual assault, and research on acquaintance and date rape.
Method: Review of literature.
Findings: Acquaintance rape is usually defined as nonconsensual sex between adults who know each other. Until recently, however, acquaintance rape was not defined as "real rape," nor was it conceptualized as a form of criminal victimization in our society. Acquaintance rape occurs in the context of dating and courtship, and it is difficult for many to see this as a situation in which rape could occur; it occurs in situations where consensual sex is a possibility; and the circumstances surrounding a date rape are frequently very different than those that characterize a stereotypical stranger rape. All of these factors make it difficult for many to define acquaintance rape as rape or as a serious incident of violent crime. Over the past decade, both public perception and laws have changed, and there has been a dramatic increase in research on acquaintance rape. There are significant

gaps in the literature, including little research on non-college populations and relatively little research on the antecedents of acquaintance rape.

6.2 Brownmiller, Susan
1975 Against Our Will: Men, Women and Rape. New York: Simon and Schuster.

Purpose: The goal of this book is to present a comprehensive analysis of the origins of rape.
Method: Critical Review.
Findings: The author reviews and critiques theories linking rape to a wide variety of social and psychological phenomena, including individual psychopathology, attitudes about sexuality, property relationships, gender socialization and stratification. Virtually all conceivable forms of rape, including rape of battle enemies, slaves, children, wives, and so on, are covered in detail. Information on the social and psychological characteristics of "typical" victims and offenders is also provided. By linking rape with property relationships and persecution of women (and sometimes men), the author makes a case for the idea that rape often has little or nothing to do with sexual desire, but is based instead on the need for power and control. The author proposes a more equitable and realistic view of the crime of rape, its victims and its perpetrators. Also addressed with regard to prevention are dangerous images of female sexuality, including pornography, in the popular culture.

6.3 Burt, Martha and Rhoda E. Estep
1981 "Who is a Victim? Definitional Problems in Sexual Victimization." Victimology 6: 15-28.

Purpose: The authors examine social factors that offer conflicting definitions of sexual assault incidents.
Method: Literature review
Findings: The social role of victim is not bestowed on all people

who have experienced a sexual assault. On a continuum of sexual interaction some people will perceive sexual assault as only those events at the extreme coercive end; others will include events on the middle of the continuum. Some feel only if the victim struggles to the maximum extent possible is it rape; all else is lumped together as just sex. Sexual assault victims face the challenge of being legitimized by society. More often that not, victims are illegitimized by cultural factors that promote competing definitions of sexual victimization. Society attempts to discredit the sexual assault victim by saying that she is lying about her experience, most likely to get back at the man accused. In the case of acquaintance rape, victims are seen as taking something that was consensual, intercourse, and turning it into something that was not consensual, rape. Even if victimization is accepted, victims are often denied the pain and damage they suffer because of the assault. The final challenge to victims is being blamed for the assault. Her experience is viewed in light of the fact that bad things happen to bad people and she must have gotten what she deserved.

6.4 Check, James V.P. and Neil Malamuth
1985 "An Empirical Assessment of Some Feminist Hypotheses about Rape." International Journal of Women's Studies 8,4:414-423.

Purpose: The study empirically examines feminist contentions about rape regarding the normality of rape; the pervasiveness of rape and sexual coercion; rape myths and their influence; and the effects of sexual violence in the mass media.
Method: The study utilizes previous research on rape.
Findings: The authors suggest that feminists have provided a useful theoretical framework for research on rape. The normality of rape theory contends that rape is a product of a sick society rather than a sick individual. As such, rape is normalized within society. Support for this theory can be found in numerous studies. The pervasiveness of rape and forced sexuality indicates that the actual number of rapes is significantly higher than what is reported

to the police. Studies on college populations indicate that this is in fact the case. Studies of rape myths and attitudes indicate that rape myths affect a variety of rape related behaviors and attitudes. Although the study of the effects of the mass media portrayal of women is a relatively new area of study, research has shown that exposure to experimental films portraying violence against women increased men's acceptance of violence against women and rape myths. The authors suggest that more research needs to be done on women's attitudes toward rape.

6.5 DeKeseredy, Walter S.
1988 "Woman Abuse in Dating Relationships: The Relevance of Social Support Theory." Journal of Family Violence 3,1:1-13.

Purpose: To describe the possible contribution of social support theory in the study of woman abuse in dating relationships.
Method: Integrative review of literature to test a model that dating is stressful and leads men to seek social support from other men and that both stress factors in dating relationships and social support increase the probability of woman abuse, and intentional physical, sexual, or psychological assaults in the relationship. Only the findings related to sexual assaults are discussed in this abstract.
Findings: Research supports the relationship between male social support and woman abuse. Both integration into male peer groups and the support functions that the male peers provide are associated with acts of woman abuse. Studies have also found support for the strong associations between both social support and stress and woman abuse. The authors conclude that there is support for their model and that social support theory is useful in explaining woman abuse in dating relationship.

6.6 Ellis, Lee
1991 "The Drive to Possess and Control as a Motivation for Sexual Behavior: Applications to

the Study of Rape." Social Science Information 30,4:663-675.

Purpose: The article seeks to contribute to the understanding of rape and other forms of violence experienced by people who know one another.
Method: A literature review of existing rape research serves as the basis of this article.
Findings: Numerous studies support the theory that humans are born with the drive to possess and control. The author suggests that this innate behavior can be applied to understanding of trauma induced bonding and date rape. Some studies have indicated that a moderate amount of women who are raped on dates continue to maintain dating relationships with the offender. This suggests that rape in dating situations may be used by men to ensure long term sex partners. If such acts are linked to innate characteristics, we may be able to reduce the incidence of such behavior.

6.7 Muehlenhard, Charlene L. and Jennifer L. Schrag
1991 "Nonviolent Sexual Coercion." Pp. 115-28 in Acquaintance Rape: The Hidden Crime, edited by Andrea Parrot and Laurie Bechhofer. New York: John Wiley and Sons.

Purpose: To review the psychological, sociological, and feminist literature on nonviolent sexual coercion. The authors argue that it is important to study the many subtle forms of coercion that lead to unwanted sex because this coercion is pervasive and has a powerful, insidious effect on women. Any unwanted sexual relation is considered to be coercive.
Method: Review of literature.
Findings: Two forms of sexual coercion are identified. Indirect sexual coercion is the pressure on women to be in male-female relationships that imply a sexual relationship. Norms about the desirability of heterosexuality, about gender roles, and about appropriate forms of sexuality are examples of indirect sexual coercion. The fear of male violence, male status dominance, and

economic inequality between men and women also contribute to the pressure on women that constitutes sexual coercion. Direct sexual coercion is the specific pressure to engage in unwanted sex in a given relationship. Forms of direct coercion are verbal pressure, which is prevalent, and coercion that is linked with the use of alcohol and drugs. An additional common form of coercion occurs when a woman indicates that she does not want to engage in sex but the man "just does it" anyway. Women face many sources of sexual coercion that are not included in the legal definition of rape. The direct forms of sexual coercion, in particular, are an important factor in understanding the prevalence of acquaintance rape.

6.8 Pineau, Lois
1989 "Date Rape: A Feminist Analysis." Law and Philosophy 8:217-243.

Purpose: To examine the legal doctrine of "reasonableness" and offer a reformulation more inclusive of the perspectives of women.
Method: Essay.
Findings: This essay breaks down many rape myths, and re-examines the philosophical foundations of much of the common law surrounding both rape and acquaintance rape. The conclusions include the incorporation of a model of "communicative sexuality," as opposed to the current "aggressive-acquiescence" model of male-female seduction. Although not empirical, this essay has some implications for re-directing both theoretical and empirical strategies.

6.9 Sanders, William B.
1980 Rape and Women's Identity. Beverly Hills: Sage.

Purpose: The goal of this book is to examine the relationship between rape and identity.
Method: Using Goffman's dramaturgic perspective, the author conceptualizes rape in terms of situational contexts, relationships,

and interaction.
Findings: The rape investigation is seen as a sort of ethnomethodology, with conclusions based on police interpretation of information and construction of the "truth." The impact of rape is described in terms of its consequences for the victim's identity. Rape prevention concepts are also discussed.

6.10 Schwendinger, Julia R. and Herman Schwendinger
1983 Rape and Inequality. Beverly Hills: Sage.

Purpose: The purpose of this research is to examine characteristics of societies which may be conducive to rape.
Method: The authors reviewed both historical and contemporary literature.
Findings: Part 1 is devoted to a review of explanations for rape, including the debunking of common rape myths and critiques of existing theories of rape. In Part 2, the authors present a perspective on rape laws as a function of a society's overall mode of production (i.e. social class relations and exploitation), rather than simple property relations between individual men and women. Part 3 links variations in violence among societies to variations in modes of production. Violence, including sexual violence, is described as a consequence of the inequalities produced by exploitative political economies. Part 4 considers changes in social conditions which may help to reduce the prevalence of rape, and emphasizes that a reduction of sexual violence is dependent upon a reduction of the overall level of violence in the society as a whole.

6.11 Shotland, Lance R.
1985 "A Preliminary Model of Some Causes of Date Rape." Academic Psychology Bulletin 7:187-200.

Purpose: This review paper proposes a typology of date rape based on gender differences in sexual interest.
Method: Research Review

Findings: The author suggests two models of date rape. "Relational" date rape arises in the course of an ongoing relationship. Men have more sexual interest than women, thus they may misinterpret their dating partner's friendliness as mutual sexual interest. "Early" date rape occurs after one or a few dates. This form may be related to a woman's frequency of dating and her reputation for promiscuity, as sexually aggressive men may find such women to be suitable targets. Men who commit early date rape may be more antisocial than other men.

6.12 Shotland, R. Lance
1989 "A Model of the Causes of Date Rape in Developing and Close Relationships." Pp. 247-270 in Close Relationships, edited by C. Hendrick. Newbury Park, CA: Sage.

Purpose: To review the literature on acquaintance rape and to develop a model of the causes of date rape.
Method: Integrative review of literature.
Findings: The author discusses three types of date rape: Beginning date rape (occurs on first few dates), Early date rape (occurs early in relationship when rules are still being established), and Relational date rape (occurs after lengthy dating and rules have been established). A model for early date rape is developed. Early date rape generally involves life style differences, miscommunication of sexual intent between men and women, certain characteristics of personality, and social attitudes. It is theorized that date rapists are more likely to overestimate the sexual intent of a dating partner. In addition, they are likely to have poor impulse control, a history of anti-social behavior, high sociopathy scores, and fewer sexual partners and aggressive acts than other types of date rapists. Victims of early date rape, on the other hand, are more likely to underestimate the sexual intent of their partner and to indicate nonconsent unassertively in later stages of foreplay. This behavior may be the result of lower assertiveness, self-esteem, and high social anxiety of the victim. Preliminary models for beginning date rape and relational date

rape are also discussed.

6.13 Shotland, R. Lance
1992 "A Theory of the Causes of Courtship Rape: Part 2." Journal of Social Issues 48,1:127-143.

Purpose: To develop a theory of courtship rape that incorporates the five types of courtship rape which occur at different stages in dating relationships.
Method: Integrative review of literature
Findings: The theory suggests that there are as many as five different types of courtship rape. Each occurs at various stages in dating relationships and involve characteristically different rapists. The first three types of rape include couples who are not sexually active. Beginning date rape occurs during the first dates and is not generally the result of miscommunication but the actions of a sexually aggressive male. Early date rape occurs after a few dates but before the establishment of sexual ground rules. Relational date rape occurs after a lengthy dating relationship and sexual ground rules have been established. The last two types of rape occur between sexually active couples. Rape occurs in both battering sexually active relationships and nonbattering sexually active relationships. There is a brief discussion of the role of rape supportive beliefs, peer support, and alcohol in date rape. Ideas about empirically testing the theoretical model are discussed.

7

ATTITUDES TOWARD ACQUAINTANCE RAPE

7.1 Barnett, Nona J. and Hubert S. Feild
1977 "Sex Differences in University Students' Attitudes Toward Rape." Journal of College and Student Personnel 18:93-96.

Purpose: The study measures the nature of the differences among university students' attitudes toward rape.
Method: Undergraduate students responded to a 25 item questionnaire that included statements such as, "A woman can not be raped against her will; women are trained by society to be rape victims; and a raped woman is less a woman."
Findings: Almost 70% of the items showed significant sex differences in attitudes toward rape. Males were more likely to attribute the motivation of rape to be sexual whereas women were more likely to attribute it to power. Similarly, males were much more concerned with protecting alleged offenders from false charges of rape. Finally, men indicate much less empathy for rape victims and more approval to rape women, with 32% indicating that it would do some women good to get raped. Although this study does not focus on acquaintance rape, per se, its population of university students makes it relevant for later work in university settings.

7.2 Bourque, Linda Brookover
1989 Defining Rape. Durham, NC: Duke University Press.

Purpose: To analyze the diversity of opinion about what constitutes rape. Bourque examines the effects of social roles on perceptions about what constitutes rape, and she examines variations in characteristics of the situation--amount of force, resistance, characteristics of the victim and offender--for their impact on perceptions.
Method: Bourque reviews the work on applying feminist theory to rape, work on men who rape, and work on attribution theory and its relevance to individual definitions of rape. Her own study is one of the few using a community, as opposed to a college, population. She sampled Los Angeles county residents in the spring and summer of 1979, and administered an interview questionnaire to measure background variables, criminal victimization experiences, attitudes about rape, and perceptions about what constitutes rape. The sample consisted of 126 whites and 125 blacks. Respondents were asked to read 32 vignettes that portrayed sexual encounters; the variables that differentiated the vignettes were force, resistance, race of male, race of female, marital status of female, occupation of male, location of encounter, and whether the male and female were acquaintances. These eight variables yielded four dimensions: relationship between victim and offender; circumstances surrounding the encounter; characteristics of the victim; and characteristics of the offender. Respondents were asked to indicate on a 6-point scale whether the situation definitely was or was not a rape.
Findings: There was a general tendency for respondents to evaluate the vignettes as probably or definitely rape. Physical force and physical resistance situations were more likely to be judged as rape. To a lesser extent, the relationship and the location were also related to judgments. Respondent characteristics interacted to some extent with information in the vignettes in affecting judgments about rape. For instance, white females relied on information about force to make their judgments, whereas black males relied more on information about resistance.

Additional results are presented regarding attitudes about rapists, causes and solutions for rape, and personal and legal definitions.

7.3 Briere, John; Neil Malamuth; and James V.P. Check
1985 "Sexuality and Rape Supportive Beliefs." International Journal of Women's Studies 8,4:398-403.

Purpose: The study attempts to determine the relationship between rape myths and other sexuality variables. Additionally the connection between self reported sexuality and endorsement of rape supportive beliefs is also examined.
Method: A male undergraduate sample responded to a 118 item questionnaire that examined their sexuality, sexual attitudes, and rape myth scales.
Findings: Those men who had an absence of a serious intimate relationship and rated sex as important were significantly more likely to not believe that a victim had been raped. Endorsement of male dominance over women was significantly associated with sexual inhibitions, increased importance of sex, and conservative sexual attitudes. Additionally, acceptance of domestic violence was significantly related to frequent use of pornography, experience with sex, and absence of significant relationships with women. The authors contend that the attitudes that are hypothesized to support rape myths are complex and that the relationship between sexual variables and rape supportive beliefs does not automatically indicates ones' proclivity to rape.

7.4 Burt, Martha
1980 "Cultural Myths and Support for Rape." Journal of Personality and Social Behavior 38,2:217-230.

Purpose: The study tests the hypothesis that acceptance of rape myths can be predicted from sex role stereotyping, adversarial sexual beliefs, sexual conservatism, and acceptance of interpersonal violence.

Method: Data were collected from interviews of 598 Minnesota adults between February and April of 1977. Households were randomly selected and interviews were conducted by experienced women from the U.S. Census Bureau. The interview contained information on the following variables: demographic information; personality variables, sex role satisfaction, self esteem, and romantic image; experience variables, intrafamilial violence, victim of an attempted or completed sexual assault, number of sexual assault victims known, and exposure to media treatments of sexual assault; and attitude variables, sex role stereotyping, sexual conservatism, adversarial sexual beliefs, and acceptance of interpersonal violence.
Findings: Acceptance of rape myths is part of an attitude structure that includes sex role stereotyping, feelings about sexuality, and acceptance of interpersonal violence. Acceptance of interpersonal violence was the strongest predictor of rape myth acceptance. Over 50% of the sample supported the beliefs that: women lie about being raped to get back at a man or to coverup an illegitimate pregnancy; "a woman who goes home with a date implies that she is willing to have sex;" and that the majority of rape victims are promiscuous or had a bad reputation sexually. Such beliefs are deeply held by many people and that such myths will be difficult to change.

7.5 Burt, Martha B.
1991 "Rape Myths and Acquaintance Rape." Pp. 26-40 in Acquaintance Rape: The Hidden Crime, edited by Andrea Parrot and Laurie Bechhofer. New York: John Wiley and Sons.

Purpose: To analyze several rape myths that serve to minimize situations in which the label of rape is applied.
Method: Review of literature.
Findings: Research has documented several common rape myths: "nothing happened," "no harm was done," "she wanted it," and "she deserved it." The cultural ideology also includes myths about men, such as the myth that only deranged men commit rape and

that men cannot control their sexual impulses. Acceptance of rape myths is associated with sex role stereotyping, adversarial sexual beliefs, sexual conservatism, and acceptance of interpersonal violence. Rape myths comprise an ideology that excuses rape and denies victims support.

7.6 Burt, Martha R. and Rochell Semmel Albin
1981 "Rape Myths, Rape Definitions, and Probability of Conviction." Journal of Applied Social Psychology 11,3:212-230.

Purpose: Using feminist analysis, this study examines how acceptance or non-acceptance of rape myths affects the definition of an act as rape, and addresses issues of cultural bias in previous research. This sheds light on the likelihood of conviction in rape cases.

Method: Subjcct were 598 adults 18+ years old. Vignettes were used in an interview setting, to manipulate variables of victim reputation, relationship between victim and assailant, and amount of force, for the expected effect on perceptions of consent. Rape-supportive attitudes were measured by scales of rape myth acceptance, adversarial sexual beliefs, and acceptance of interpersonal violence.

Findings: Higher levels of rape myth acceptance and a greater likelihood to believe the victim precipitated the act reduced the probability that an act would be defined as rape. The assailant's intent to commit rape, the use of force, and lack of choice for the victim increase the likelihood of a rape definition. Acceptance of interpersonal violence, beliefs concerning victim precipitation, and a "desire to know more in general and more about the defendant's character in particular" reduced the likelihood of conviction. Positive evaluations of the male in the vignette reduced the probability of a rape definition, while positive perceptions of the woman had the opposite effect. Overall, the authors found that "the breadth or narrowness of rape definitions depend in part on the rape-supportive attitudes held by the general public."

7.7 Check, James V.P. and Neil M. Malamuth
1983 "Sex Role Stereotyping and Reactions to Depictions of Stranger Versus Acquaintance Rape." Journal of Personality and Social Psychology 45,2:344-356.

Purpose: The study tests the hypothesis that sex role stereotyping and the situational context in which rape is portrayed affect people's reactions to rape.
Method: Undergraduate students responded to a questionnaire that measured their sex role stereotyping and attitudes about sex and violence. In the second phase of the study, subjects were placed in an experimental context where they were presented with one of three sexually explicit descriptions. They were asked to indicate their perceptions of the depictions and their sexual arousal. Additionally, men were asked to indicate their own likelihood of acting as the man in the story did.
Findings: Those subjects who have low sex role stereotyping showed inhibited sexual arousal to the rape depiction as compared to the consenting sex depiction. On the other hand, high sex role adherence subjects exhibited equal sexual arousal levels to both the consenting and rape depictions. In fact, these subjects showed higher, although not significant, arousal to the acquaintance rape scenario. These patterns are similar to those of identified rapists. All subjects indicated that the woman in both the stranger and acquaintance rape scenarios were less favorable than the woman in the consenting scenario. Over 30% of the men indicate some likelihood of raping. High sex role stereotyping men indicated a higher likelihood of raping than low sex role stereotyping men.

7.8 Clark, Lorenne M. G. and Debra J. Lewis.
1977 Rape: The Price of Coercive Sexuality. Toronto: The Women's Press.

Purpose: The goal of this research was to better understand the social arrangements which perpetuate the commission of rape.
Method: The sample consisted of all cases of completed rape

reported to the Metropolitan Toronto Police Department in the year 1970. Only nonmarital rapes of women over age 14 were included in the analysis. This led to 116 cases involving 117 victims and 129 offenders.
Findings: Part I of the book describes the study methodology and major findings. The authors suggest that the number of rapes classified by the police as "unfounded" was overestimated, based on legal loopholes and personal/professional biases. For example, the proportions of cases classified as unfounded were much higher when the rapist was known to the victim, when the victim had been drinking prior to the assault, and when the offender had a weapon. Characteristics of victims and rapists are also described in this section. Part II offers a theoretical perspective on rape with which to understand the study findings. The authors propose that attitudes about male and female sexuality and inequitable social relationships between men and women lead to a variety of justifications for blaming rape victims for their own misfortunes. When women are viewed as the property of men, rape laws serve not to protect women from rape, but to protect men from crimes against their "property." Rape needs to be viewed as a serious crime against one's person (such as physical assault) if it is to be properly dealt with by society. The authors offer recommendations for social change which may help to reduce the incidence of rape.

7.9 Dull, Thomas R. and David J. Giacopassi
1987 "Demographic Correlates of Sexual and Dating Attitudes, a Study of Date Rape." Criminal Justice and Behavior 14,2:175-193.

Purpose: The study examines attitudes toward to sex, dating, and date rape in relation to demographic variables of sex, race, age, and religiosity.
Method: Undergraduate students responded to a 15 item questionnaire that measured attitudes toward sex, dating, sexual aggression, and rape.
Findings: There was a strong awareness on campus that date rape

is a common occurrence. However, there were large disparities between attitudes of men compared to women. Aggressive attitudes toward sex, dating, and rape were strongly held by male respondents. For example, compared to women, men were more likely to agree with statements that hold the man as the aggressor and the woman as the prey in dating relationships. Men were also more likely to indicate that physical aggression is a necessary prelude of love; and females who frequently ask males out on dates are probably looking for sex; and that rape by a stranger should be viewed as more serious than by an acquaintance. When examining responses according to race, blacks in comparison to whites were more likely to indicate that males are expected to be the aggressor in sexual relation with women; most men would rape if they were certain that nobody would know; and a female cannot be forced to have sex against her will. On the other hand, blacks were also more likely to reject attitudes that females who ask males out are looking for sex and that normal males do not commit rape. No significant age and religiosity differences were found.

7.10 Feltey, Kathryn M.; Julie J. Ainslie; and Aleta Geib
1991 "Sexual Coercion Attitudes among High School Students: The Influence of Gender and Rape Education." Youth and Society 23,2:229-250.

Purpose: To add to the research on sexual aggression which has largely focused on college students by studying younger students in high school and seeking to understand the development of attitudes about sexual aggression during adolescence. Also, to analyze the effects of gender and structural and individual-level factors, including a date rape prevention program, on the attitudes of adolescents.
Method: 378 students from urban, suburban, and rural high schools completed a pretest survey before attending a lecture on date rape prevention which was presented by local YMCA Rape Crisis Programs. Then, a subgroup of 118 students from a suburban high school were posttested. The surveys collected data

on demographic characteristics, sexual activity, and attitudes about sexual coercion under different conditions.

Findings: One-fifth of the students reported that they had sex when they did not want to. Women's involuntary sex is a result of coercion while men's is a result of peer group pressure. Before Date Rape Prevention Program: Men were significantly more likely than women to approve of sexual coercion across all situations. Age was also significantly related to support of sexual coercion. Support decreases as subjects age. After the Date Rape Prevention Program: Men and women differed in support of sexual coercion only under certain situations: when the woman creates an opportunity for sexual activity and there is an established relationship. Overall, gender was no longer a powerful factor in explaining support of sexual coercion. The effects of age remained significant. The most significant factor in explaining support of sexual coercion is unwilling sexual experience. Those subjects who had experienced unwanted sexual activity were more likely to support sexual coercion in certain situations. Thus, it is concluded that those adolescents who were coerced into sex are more likely to perceive sexual coercion as normative. Overall, the Date Rape Prevention program is successful in decreasing gender differences in support of sexual coercion.

7.11 Fischer, Gloria J.

1986 "College Student Attitudes Toward Forcible Date Rape: I. Cognitive Predictors." Archives of Sexual Behavior 15,6:457-466.

Purpose: The study measures undergraduate students' acceptance of forcible date rape, attitudes toward women, sexual knowledge, sexual experience, tolerance of socially unapproved sexual behavior, and religiosity.

Method: In the fall of 1982, 278 undergraduate students responded to a 54 item survey that measured gender, age, class in school, tolerance of socially unapproved sexual behavior, sexual experience, religiosity, sexual knowledge, attitudes toward women, and attitudes toward date rape. In the fall of 1983, 283 students

responded to a 63 item survey that measured gender, age, class, number of younger sisters, sexual tolerance, sexual experience, religiosity, sexual knowledge, attitudes toward women, and attitudes towards date rape.
Findings: Subjects who held less rejecting attitudes toward forcible date rape were less sure that rape is really rape and tend to have more traditional attitudes toward women. They are also more tolerant of socially unapproved sexual behaviors and have less accurate sexual knowledge. Religiosity and sexual experience did not correlate with acceptance of forcible date rape.

7.12 Fischer, Gloria J.
1986 "College Student Attitudes Toward Forcible Date Rape: Changes After Taking a Human Sexuality Course." Journal of Sex Education and Therapy 12:42-46.

Purpose: To examine how a course in Human Sexuality changed students sexual attitudes, knowledge, experiences, and attitudes toward women, as these were considered the best predictors of attitudes towards forcible date rape.
Method: A survey was administered to undergraduates in three Human Sexuality classes at the beginning and end of the course. The survey measured sexual attitudes, experience, religiosity, sexual knowledge, and a forcible date rape vignette, which was followed by questions concerning attitudes toward date rape. The exam was also administered to one section of Introductory Psychology, in which the topic of rape was not covered. This was repeated one year later.
Findings: In the survey at the beginning of each class the scores were comparable. The behavior of the male in the date rape scenario was viewed less favorably in the post-class test only among subjects in the Human Sexuality class. A gender interaction was seen in one section of the Human Sexuality students, where the males changed to an absolutely opposite attitude toward the vignette (they considered the male's behavior absolutely more acceptable). The author notes that in this class

alone was a confrontational approach to the subject taken, and these responses may reflect a defensive reaction-formation. Women, but not men, became more certain that the male's behavior constituted rape. This was also found among the Introductory Psych students. Sexual knowledge increased significantly among students in the Human Sexuality class. The results of the second years surveys were almost identical. The author concludes by citing this as evidence of the mediating effects of a Human Sexuality course on date rape attitudes.

7.13 Fischer, Gloria
1987 "Hispanic and Majority Student Attitudes Toward Forcible Date Rape as a Function of Differences in Attitudes Toward Women." Sex Roles 17,1/2:93-101.

Purpose: The study tests the hypothesis that bicultural and bilingual Hispanic students will hold more traditional attitudes toward women and will have less rejecting attitudes toward forcible date rape.
Method: Undergraduate student responded to a 61 item survey that measured the following variables: demographics such as gender, ethnic origin, age, etc; attitudes toward socially unapproved sexual behavior; sexual experience; religiosity; sexual knowledge; and perceptions of whether a description of date rape is considered rape. Additionally, two question assessed bilingual ability and bicultural background.
Findings: Hispanic students indicated that they were more religious and had more traditional attitudes toward women than other students. In support of the hypothesis, Hispanic students were less likely to view the male's behavior in the date rape scenario as unacceptable, were less tolerant of socially unapproved sexual behavior, and had less sexual knowledge than other students. Several significant gender differences surfaced regarding the attribution of blame. White females were less likely than white males to blame the male in the date rape scenario and more likely to blame society. There were no differences among

Hispanic males and females regarding attribution of blame. However, there were significant differences regarding attitudes of forcible date rape. Bicultural and bilingual Hispanic women were less rejecting of forcible date rape attitudes than assimilated Hispanics and white women. Hispanic males, regardless of their ethnic assimilation were less rejecting of forcible date rape than were white males. These differences suggest the need to expand the meaning of Hispanic in research differences.

7.14 Garrett-Gooding, Joy and Richard Senter, Jr.
1987 "Attitudes and Acts of Sexual Aggression on a University Campus." Sociological Inquiry 57:349-371.

Purpose: To investigate whether men and women, given a traditional sex-role definitions, will be more likely to judge the physical sexual coercion of women as acceptable. It is hypothesized that men who are strongly traditional in their sex-role beliefs will be more likely than other men to engage in sexual aggression toward women.
Method: Subjects were 778 university undergraduates. They filled out a questionnaire, from which four main indexes were derived: Frequency of men's Sexual Coercion, Frequency/Severity of men's Sexual Coercion, Frequency of women's Sexual Victimization, and Frequency/Severity of women's Sexual Victimization.
Findings: The data strongly supported the hypothesis that traditional sex-role orientation coincides with higher level of acceptability for physical coercion. Men who are traditionally identified were more likely to engage in sexual coercion. No relationship was found between class standing and acceptance of coercion. However, a moderate relationship was found between fraternity membership and attitudes towards coercion, suggesting a socializing effect. No relationship was found between victimization and sorority membership, though. The authors also note that the men surveyed may be admitting to less coercion than occurs given the woman's levels of victimization. Part of this may be explained if a minority of the men are repeat offenders.

7.15 Giacopassi, David and R. Thomas Dull
1986 "Gender and Racial Differences in the Acceptance of Rape Myths Within a College Population." Sex Roles 15,1/2:63-75.

Purpose: To measure the acceptance of rape myths associated with rape, rape victims, and rapists. This study is not about acquaintance rape in particular. It is included because of the relevance of some of the rape myths studied and because of its college sample.
Method: Undergraduate students responded to a questionnaire that measured acceptance or rejection of statements reflecting rape myths.
Findings: Respondents were more likely to reject myths that reflect negatively on themselves and thus are more likely to accept myths that blame some other racial or sexual group. the findings support the "Just World" concept. Black males were the most accepting of rape myths, perceiving rape as an unplanned, spontaneous event rather than a premeditated criminal behavior. Black women, compared to white women, see both the rape victim and the offender as blame worthy and are more likely to believe that women cannot be forced to have sex against their will; that women fantasize about rape; and that victims of rape are frequently to blame for the crime. This study is not about acquaintance rape in particular. It is included because of the relevance of some of the rape myths studied and because of its college sample.

7.16 Gilmartin-Zena, Pat
1988 "Gender Differences in Students' Attitudes Toward Rape." Sociological Focus 21:279-292.

Purpose: To develop and test a new instrument for measuring rape myth acceptance, and to examine attitudes and potential gender differences in attitudes about rape among college students.
Method: The instrument developed in the study included 24 rape myths gathered through analysis of the rape literature. The myths

fall into the following categories: (1) women's causal role in rape, (2) motives of the assailant, (3) seriousness of rape, (4) characteristics of the assault, (5) characteristics of the victim, and (6) structural factors thought to cause rape. A questionnaire including this new measure was distributed and completed by 198 (68 men, 130 women) undergraduate students.
Findings: Results show that the students tended to believe several of the rape myths, especially those that concerning the causes of rape. Specifically, woman's causal role was widely accepted. There were gender differences in the acceptance of race myths. Men were more likely than women to accept all of the rape myths items. This study is indirectly relevant to acquaintance rape since several of the rape myths deal with acquaintance situations. The college sample also makes the study relevant to later work on acquaintance rape.

7.17 Goodchilds, J.D. and G.L. Zellman
1984 "Sexual Signaling and Sexual Aggression in Adolescent Relationships." Pp. 233-243 in Pornography and Sexual Aggression, edited by N.M. Malamuth and E. Donnerstein. Orlando, FL: Academic Press.

Purpose: To examine the extent to which sexual "signaling" among adolescents has changed, to reflect societal-level changes toward more egalitarian gender relations. One particular aspect of "signaling" concerns nonconsensual sex, and this aspect of the paper is relevant for acquaintance rape.
Method: Interviews with 432 14-18 year olds. Vignettes were used to measure the variables relevant for acquaintance rape. These were varied by setting, relationship between the male and female, and the type of pressure used by the male. Respondents were asked who was responsible for the nonconsensual sex, whether they liked the boy and girl described in the vignette, whether the sex was rape, and whether the girl in the vignette would want to see the boy again. Respondents were also asked

"Under what circumstances is it OK for a guy to hold a girl down and force her to have sexual intercourse?"

Findings: Setting had no relationship with any of the outcome variables. Surprisingly, there was little impact of gender on responses. Most of the responsibility for what happened was assigned to the boy, although the nonconsenting girl was also held somewhat responsible. The male was seen as most responsible when he used force. Those vignettes characterized by force were most likely to be evaluated as rape. Although 72% of the respondents claimed there were no circumstances in which a boy was justified in holding a girl down and forcing intercourse, when asked about specific situations, more respondents stated that the boy would be justified. The authors conclude that "while the extent to which male adolescents accept sexual assault as justified is surprising, the numbers of female adolescents who also condone a male attack is truly astounding."

7.18 Gordon, Margaret T. and Stephanie Riger
1991 The Female Fear: The Social Cost of Rape. Chicago: University of Illinois.

Purpose: The authors' goal is to describe and explain women's fears about rape.

Method: This study was based on archival research, personal interviews with women, and a telephone survey of 4,073 adults,

Findings: The authors focus primarily upon women's fears about rape by strangers. However, they do address acquaintance rape in several places. Chapter 3 provides a brief overview of various forms of rape. Chapter 5 provides a historical discussion of the social origins of women's rape fears. Chapter 6 contains a review of legal issues. Chapter 7 discusses the role of the media, including pornography, in exploiting women's fear of rape. Chapter 10 considers policy avenues for rape prevention and public education strategies.

7.19 Johnson, James D. and Lee A. Jackson, Jr.
1988 "Assessing the Effects of Factors that Might Underlie the Differential Perception of Acquaintance and Stranger Rape." Sex Roles 19,1/2:37-45.

Purpose: To assess the perceptual effects of factors that might underlie the tendency to view acquaintance rape victims less favorably, and the perpetrator more leniently, than in a stranger rape. Victim/perpetrator attraction and ambiguity in the victim's desire for intercourse were the primary variables.
Method: The subjects were 60 male and 60 female undergraduate students. Each subject read a passage concerning a forced sexual encounter that varied by attraction (minimal, moderate, maximal) and victim desire (ambiguous, relatively unambiguous). They were then instructed to answer several question concerning the rape (female responsibility, male responsibility, male's intention to harm, probability of guilt in court, and if guilty, appropriate sentence).
Findings: In both ambiguous and unambiguous scenarios, the perpetrator was seen as more responsible for the rape. However, as the situation became more ambiguous, the victims "share" of responsibility increased. The subjects regarded him less likely to be found guilty in the ambiguous situation. There was a significant subject gender interaction, with males attributing more responsibility to the victim than females. No other main effects were seen.

7.20 Johnson, James D. and Inger Russ
1989 "Effects of Salience of Consciousness-Raising Information on Perceptions of Acquaintance versus Stranger Rape." Journal of Applied Psychology 19:1182-97.

Purpose: To examine the factors which may alter biased rape perceptions, the effects of salient consciousness raising information on perceptions of rape, and further develop research on the differences between perceptions of acquaintance and stranger rape. Method: The experiment was performed using a sample of 80 men and 80 women undergraduate students. The subjects were randomly assigned to one of eight conditions. The experiment was divided into three parts. First, the subjects were randomly assigned to listen to and give their impressions of a speech. The salient condition consisted of a speech on the mistreatment of women in America. Then, the subjects listened and gave impression of three instrumental songs (irrelevant in analysis). Finally, they read written passages. The subjects were randomly assigned to one of two conditions which varied in whether they depicted an acquaintance rape or stranger rape. After reading the passages, subjects responded to questions about their impressions including probability that the woman received enjoyment, woman's responsibility, and likelihood that male subjects would exhibit similar behavior if they wouldn't get caught.

Findings: Subjects in nonsalient condition (did not hear speech on mistreatment of women) attributed significantly more responsibility to the victim than subjects in the salient condition. Furthermore, men in nonsalient condition were significantly more likely to report that they would rape if they would not get caught. When comparing the differences between perceptions of acquaintance and stranger rape, it was found that the subjects in the acquaintance rape condition perceived the victim as more likely to be enjoying the assault and to be more responsible than those in stranger rape condition. It was also found that men in acquaintance rape condition were more likely to report that they would commit rape than those in stranger rape condition. There were gender difference in perceptions of the victim. Men were more likely than women to perceive the victim as receiving enjoyment. Thus, it is concluded that perceptions of rape can be altered by factors such as salience of consciousness-raising information, type of rape, and gender. Salience of consciousness-raising information did appear to be successful in developing more favorable perceptions of the victim and lower reports of likelihood to commit rape in men.

7.21 Kanin, Eugene; Eugene Jackson; and Edward M. Levine
1987 "Personal Sexual History and Punitive Judgements for Rape." Psychological Reports 61:439-442.

Purpose: To examine the effects of sexual histories on views of the seriousness of rape.
Method: Questionnaires were distributed and completed by 355 undergraduate students (155 men and 200 women). The subjects were asked to read a vignette describing a case of acquaintance rape and then judge the seriousness of the assault.
Findings: Results show a significant relationship between the number of partners an individual has had and their recommended length of prison sentence. For both men and women, as the number of sexual partners increased, the mean number of years of imprisonment recommended for the perpetrator decreased. Thus, it is concluded that individuals who are more sexually active perceive rape to be a less serious crime. This finding is further supported by results that show that as the number of partners increases, there is an increase in the belief that when there has been prior intimacy a rape has not occurred. This relationship holds for both men and women, however, men are more likely to hold these beliefs.

7.22 L'Armand, K. and A. Pepitone
1982 "Judgements of Rape: A Study of Victim-Rapist Relationship and Victim Sexual History." Personality and Social Psychology Bulletin 8,1:134-139.

Purpose: To examine the prediction that perceptions of the seriousness of a rape will be inversely related to the victim's past sexual history, and that it will be judged less-serious if the victim and rapist have a dating or intimate relationship.
Method: The subjects were 650 university students, 60% men and 40% women. They were instructed to read a news story of a rape trial and conviction, varied by sexual history of the victim (no mention, one previous experience, many previous experiences),

and by relationship (strangers, dating, dating with previous consensual intercourse). They were then to recommend a sentence (0-50 years), rate the seriousness of the crime (0-100), and reply to the question, "Why did you recommend the sentence you did?". The last question was scored for major theme.
Findings: Even where the use of force was clearly established, the judgements of seriousness were affected by perceptions of chastity and the victim/rapist relationship, in the hypothesized directions. Significant gender differences were found, women tending to view the rape as a more serious offense than men. The authors proposed further research, considering the "damage" hypothesis. More than a simple causal relationship, they suggest that the seriousness may be perceived in terms of damage, with a chaste victim suffering more harm than an unchaste victim.

7.23 Lewin, Miriam
1985 "Unwanted Intercourse: The Difficulty of Saying No." Psychology of Women Quarterly 9:184-192.

Purpose: The author interviewed women about their experience with unwanted intercourse in order to develop hypotheses about the phenomenon.
Method: 76 undergraduate women were shown videotaped vignettes, including one depicting a potentially coercive date situation, and asked to write two stories: one in which the woman refuses sex, and one in which the woman agrees to sex. Each subject also completed a structured questionnaire about how the man would feel, and how she would feel as the woman in the vignette, under both the intercourse and no intercourse conditions.
Findings: A cost-benefit analysis revealed that concern about the man being hurt by the woman's refusal helped to mitigate some subjects' negative feelings about the acceptance condition. Most subjects wrote stories which ended negatively when the woman agreed to sex, and positively when she refused sex, but subjects with prior unwanted sexual experiences were more likely to write stories which ended negatively under both conditions. The vast

majority of subjects felt the relationship would end if the woman refused sex. The author proposes four cultural norms which explain the persistence of unwanted sex.

7.24 Malamuth, Neil M. and James V.P. Check
1980 "Sexual Arousal to Rape and Consenting Depictions: The Importance of the Woman's Arousal." Journal of Abnormal Psychology 89,6:763-766.

Purpose: The objective of this research was to identify aspects of rape scenarios which inhibit arousal in a nonrapist sample.
Method: A factorial survey was administered to 143 male and female undergraduates.
Findings: Subjects were significantly more aroused by a rape vignette when the woman was described as experiencing sexual arousal than when she was described as experiencing disgust. No significant effects on subject arousal were noted for the two other variables, woman's consent and woman's experience of pain.

Malamuth's work in the early 1980s does not deal specifically with acquaintance rape since it predates the separate conceptualization of acquaintance rape. However, it is work that became very important in that conceptualization, since it emphasizes the proclivity to rape and the "normality" of rapists. His work on rape depictions is included because of its influence on later developments.

7.25 Malamuth, Neil M.; Scott Haber; and Seymour Feshbach

1980 "Testing Hypotheses Regarding Rape: Exposure to Sexual Violence, Sex Differences, and the 'Normality' of Rapists." Journal of Research in Personality 14:121-137.

Purpose: The goals of this research were (1) to determine whether exposure to violent porn affects sexual arousal to rape depictions and whether this arousal varies by gender, and (2) to gauge perceptions regarding women's enjoyment of rape and men's rape proclivity.

Method: 91 male and female undergraduates were administered a questionnaire and asked to read two vignettes: first, a pornographic story (either violent or nonviolent); then, a depiction of rape.

Findings: Men who had read the violent version of the pornographic story were more aroused by the rape depiction, but were also more punitive towards the fictional rapist. Overall, men who had read the violent pornography were less sensitive to the effects of the rape on the victim than men who had read the nonviolent version. However, among men who had read the violent pornography, those with high scores for aggression-anxiety were more sensitive to the effects of the rape on the victim than those with low aggression-anxiety scores. Descriptions of the victim's pain were generally associated with lower sexual arousal to the rape depiction for all subjects, but for men who had read the violent pornography, greater pain was associated with greater sexual arousal. Overall, women identified more with the victim, and were more punitive to the rapist, than men. Subjects believed that about 25% of women would experience some pleasure in being raped, although almost no women reported that they personally would enjoy being raped. Subjects estimated that about 50% of men would commit rape if they knew they wouldn't be caught, and the same percentage of male subjects indicated that they might commit a rape under those circumstances.

7.26 Malamuth, Neil M.; Maggie Heim; and Seymour Feshbach
1980 "Sexual Responsiveness of College Students to Rape Depictions: Inhibitory and Disinhibitory Effects." Journal of Personality and Social Psychology 38,3:399-408.

Purpose: The purpose of this research was to identify characteristics of a rape depiction which lead to sexual arousal,

and those which inhibit arousal, in a nonrapist sample.
Method: Two experiments were conducted: (1) 308 undergraduates read a vignette in which several dimensions (including rape vs nonrape) were manipulated, and then rated their own arousal; and (2) 128 undergraduates read only the rape versions of the vignettes used in Experiment 1, with an additional manipulation added (the woman's experience of disgust and nausea vs pleasure and orgasm) and then rated their own arousal.
Findings: In the first experiment, subjects were more likely to be aroused by the mutually consenting version of the story than by the rape version regardless of whether the woman was described as experiencing pain, the man's actions were described as aggressive, or the man's motive was to abuse the woman. Subjects who read the rape version were more likely to feel angry or offended as a result. Among those who had read the rape version, females were more likely than males to feel angry and offended. This experiment suggests that normals are less likely to be turned on by rape depictions than by non-rape depictions, but because none of the other effects were significant, it sheds little light on the broader question of why non-rape pornography with assaultive themes (e.g. woman's pain) is often sexually arousing while rape porn typically is not.

In the second experiment, subjects were more likely to be turned on when the woman experienced orgasm than when she experienced nausea. Female subjects were most aroused when the depiction included woman's orgasm and lack of pain, while men were most turned on by the combination of orgasm and pain. Suggests that men may be turned on by the control feature of a situation involving orgasm despite pain. Overall, subjects reported fewer negative feelings (e.g. anger, anxiety) when the woman experienced orgasm than when she experienced nausea, and more negative feelings when the woman was described as experiencing pain. Suggests that descriptions of woman's pleasure mitigates inhibiting effect of violent pornography.

7.27 Margolin, Leslie; Melody Miller; and Patricia Moran
1989 "When a Kiss is Not Just a Kiss: Relating Violations of Consent in Kissing to Rape Myth Acceptance." Sex Roles 20:231-243.

Purpose: To examine the relationship between attitudes about violations in consent to kissing and rape myth acceptance.
Method: Questionnaires were distributed and completed by 162 female and 49 male undergraduate students. The subjects were randomly assigned to one of three groups. Each group read a vignette depicting a nonconsensual kiss, but received a different description of the relationship between the couple: married, "going together," or first date. Then, the subjects were asked to rate the acceptability of the woman's right to refuse the kiss and the man's right to ignore her refusal on a 7-point Likert type scale.
Findings: Results show that there is a strong relationship between gender and rape myth acceptance. Rape myth acceptance had the strongest effect on approval of violations in consent to kissing. Gender was also related. Men reported much greater acceptance of the man's right to ignore the woman's refusal, but there was not a gender difference in attitudes towards the woman's right to refuse. However, when considering the specific myths, variation was found in the correlations of the 19 rape myths to attitudes about the vignette and gender. Open-ended responses reveal more information about gender differences in approval of violations in consent to kissing. Women had emotional reactions, while men tended to be unemotional.

7.28 McKinney, Kathleen
1986 "Perceptions of Courtship Violence: Gender Difference and Involvement." Free Inquiry in Creative Sociology 14,1:61-66.

Purpose: To review the literature on attitudes related to courtship violence, to examine gender differences in attitudes of courtship violence, and to analyze the relationship between attitudes and involvement in courtship violence.

Method: A self administered questionnaire was distributed and completed by 163 students (78 men and 85 women) gathered through volunteer convenience sampling at Oklahoma State University. Data were gathered on demographic characteristics, abuse in family of origin, personal definitions of, involvement in, and attitudes towards courtship violence. Involvement in courtship violence was measured using a 2 part measure developed from unstructured interviews. Attitudes about courtship violence were measured using a 25 item version of the Attitudes Towards Women Scale (AWS), a 12 item Courtship Violence Scale (CVS), and other questions about frequency, seriousness, and blame of courtship violence. Only the findings about sexual courtship violence are discussed in this abstract.

Findings: A significant gender difference was not found on the total courtship violence scale, but women were significantly more likely than men to disagree with the two items concerning sexual violence: "Your steady partner has the right to have sex with you anytime it is wanted" and "Sexual dating violence is not a serious problem." There were not many significant correlations between courtship violence attitudes and involvement. However, men with liberal attitudes towards women reported perpetrating significantly more sexual violence against women and women with more liberal attitudes towards women reported significantly more experiences as victims of sexual dating violence. A possible explanation is that liberal men may have expectations of more sexual activity by women and liberal women may engage in behaviors that increase the risk of violence, such as going to bars. However, it is suggested that more research need to be performed to clarify and improve previous studies.

7.29 Muehlenhard, Charlene L.
1988 "Misinterpreted Dating Behaviors and the Risk of Date Rape." Journal of Social and Clinical Psychology 6,1:20-37.

Purpose: The goals of this research were to (1) examine gender differences in interpretation of dating behaviors and in assessments

of the justifiability of date rape, and (2) to determine the impact of traditional beliefs about rape justifiability and a woman's desire for sex.
Method: 540 undergraduates each completed the Attitudes Towards Women Scale, read 11 dating vignettes, and then rated the woman's willingness to have sex and the justifiability of the man's forcing her to have sex.
Findings: Subjects were more likely to believe that the woman wanted sex and that the rape was justifiable when the couple went to the man's apartment (rather than a movie or a religious function), when the woman initiated the date, and when the man paid all of the expenses. Males were more likely than females to believe that the woman wanted sex, and that the rape was justifiable, across almost all of the dating scenarios. Subjects with traditional ATW were more likely to believe that the woman wanted to have sex when she initiated the date, and more likely to believe the rape was justifiable across all situations, than those with nontraditional attitudes.

7.30 Muehlenhard, Charlene L.; Debra E. Friedman; and Celeste M. Thomas
1985 "Is Date Rape Justifiable? The Effects of Dating Activity, Who Initiated, Who Paid, and Men's Attitudes toward Women." Psychology of Women Quarterly 9: 297-310.

Purpose: The authors' purpose was to determine what factors account for attitudes which justify rape.
Method: The research included two studies: (1) 100 students read a questionnaire containing 11 vignettes about hypothetical date rapes and rated the justifiability of each; and (2) 168 students read a series of vignettes, each of which was followed by a scale of sexual behaviors; for each behavior students rated how much the woman in the vignette expected the behavior, how willing she was to engage in that behavior, and whether the man would be justified in engaging in the behavior against the woman's will. Subjects in study 2 also completed the Attitudes Towards Women scale.

Findings: Subjects' ratings of the justifiability of forced sex, the woman's willingness to engage in such acts, and her expectation of such actions were all lower if the date was at a religious function vs the man's apartment. In Study 1, the woman's expectation of forced sex was highest when she initiated the date; in Study 2, the woman's expectations and the justifiability of forced sex were highest when she initiated the date and the date was at the man's apartment. In Study 1, rape was more justifiable if the man had paid for the date. Justifibaility of rape was higher among traditional men. For all but one pair of behaviors, each behavior on the Sexual Experiences Scale was rated as more expected, more willingly engaged in, and more justifiable than the one preceding it.

7.31 Sandberg, Genell; Thomas L. Jackson; and Patricia Petretic-Jackson
1987 "College Students' Attitudes Regarding Sexual Coercion and Aggression: Developing Educational and Preventive Strategies." Journal of College Student Development 28:302-311.

Purpose: To survey attitudes about sexual activities and dating issues among college students, and examine the incidence of sexual coercion and aggression.
Method: Participants were 408 undergraduate students, 247 women and 161 men. Each completed a 13-item questionnaire to examine attitudes about sexual activity during dating as well as the respondent's experiences. Each item was scored on a 6-point scale, from never (1) to frequently (6).
Findings: The findings support their hypothesis that the dating situation as a whole is an ambiguous one that may result in physically and sexually coercive behavior by either partner. About 60% of all respondents believed that dating partners provoked sexually aggressive behavior by refusing requests. 87% reported excessively jealous or possessive partners. About half believed that sexual activity was expected of them after an expensive date. Significantly more men felt that a dating partner said "no" when

they meant "yes." Significantly more women reported being verbally pressured, sexually assaulted, sexually abused, physically abused, and being forced to have intercourse. However, women were still more comfortable saying "no" to sexual activity. The authors closed the article with some preventive and educational strategies.

7.32 Schultz, LeRoy G. and Jan DeSavage
1975 "Rape and Rape Attitudes on a College Campus." Pp. 77-88 in Rape Victimology, edited by LeRoy Schultz. Springfield, IL: Charles C. Thomas.

Purpose: The purpose of this study was to establish the frequency and severity of acquaintance rape on a college campus, and to assess students' attitudes about it.
Method: 50 undergraduates completed a mail questionnaire which included a scale of sexual violence on which subjects were asked to indicate the level which constituted a "legal" rape. The instrument also contained items regarding victim precipitation, resistance strategies, and response to being raped.
Findings: The authors found that 26% of females reported being raped at least once, and 20% of males reported at least one experience with forced sodomy. 70% of the victimized females had successfully used some resistance strategy, while 24% had refrained from resisting in an effort to avoid injury. Non-victimized females were most likely to report that, if raped, their first action would be to notify the police. However, victimized females were more likely to report that they attended to their health needs first, while none of the victimized males had reported the assault to anyone. Victimized females were most likely, and males least likely, to correctly identify the legal parameters of rape. Males were more likely than females to define forced sex as rape when foreplay had occurred but the woman changed her mind at the last minute. Previously victimized females were much more likely than non-victimized females to believe that sometimes women provoke a rape; however, no overall gender differences were noted. Men, non-victimized women, and previously

victimized women all differed in their definitions of consent to sexual intercourse. The authors call for increased rape prevention instruction and rape crisis services on college campuses, and increased attention to victim needs by the court system.

7.33 Shotland, R. Lance and Lynne Goodstein
1992 "Sexual Precedence Reduces the Perceived Legitimacy of Sexual Refusal: An Examination of Attributions Concerning Date Rape and Consensual Sex." Journal of Personality and Social Psychology 18:756-764.

Purpose: To examine the effects of sexual precedence on sexual behavior.
Method: The experiment involved a sample of 357 subjects (180 men and 177 women). Each subject was randomly assigned to read a vignette describing a sexually aggressive act between dating partners within one of twelve contexts. The 12 versions of the vignettes differed in the extent of sexual experience of the dating couple and the number of prior sexual partners each member of the couple had. Then, each subject responded to questions about the vignette on a 5-point Likert type scale. The questions were concerned with the woman's attitudes and behavior (measured using Women's Intent Scale, Women's Protest Scale, and Sexual Contract Scale), man's behavior after woman's protest (measured using Rape Scale and Violence Scale), and sexual respectability of the partners (measured using Sexual Respectability of the Male, Respectability of the Female). A second experiment containing a similar design was conducted focusing on sexual precedence and consensual sexual activity.
Findings: Prior sexual involvement of dating couple was related to a belief in a sexual contract and perceptions of dating violence. If a woman has had even ten prior sexual experiences with her partner, it is perceived that she does not have the right to refuse sex and sexual violence is perceived as less serious and damaging. There was a significant difference between women and men on the idea of a sexual contract. Men were more likely to believe that

prior sexual encounters reduce the woman's right to refuse sex. It is concluded that these findings support the lack of state laws against marital rape which view women as sexual property of their partners.

7.34 Stanko, Elizabeth Anne
1987 "Ordinary Fear: Women, Violence, and Personal Safety." Pp. 155-164 in Violence Against Women: The Bloody Footprints, edited by Pauline Bart and Eileen Geil Moran. Newbury Park, CA: Sage.

Purpose: This review paper addresses women's fear of crime.
Method: Research Review.
Findings: Much of women's fear about crime centers on rape. The author proposes that women's fear of crime translates to a fear of men. Women take more precautions to ensure their own personal safety than men do. Precautions extend beyond potential encounters with stranger assailants; women also negotiate their safety with male acquaintances at work, in social situations, and at home. Most self-defense and crime prevention programs fail to address the fact that women may be most unsafe with men whom they know.

7.35 White, Jacquelyn W. and John A. Humphrey
1991 "Young People's Attitudes Toward Acquaintance Rape." Pp. 43-56 in Acquaintance Rape: The Hidden Crime, edited by Andrea Parrot and Laurie Bechhofer. New York: John Wiley and Sons.

Purpose: To analyze the social context within which young people's attitudes toward acquaintance rape develop. Although young people share the cultural belief that rape is an abhorrent form of violence, they also tend to accept forced sexual activity between acquaintances as normative, and not as rape.

Method: Review of literature.
Findings: The consensus among young adults is that forced sexual activity is expected. They are reluctant to use the rape label, particularly if the man and woman involved are dating each other. If force is involved, the rape label is more likely to be invoked. Other variables that affect whether forced sex is labelled rape are the woman's dress, location of date, use of alcohol or drugs, reputations, amount of money spent on the date, the man's level of sexual arousal, and level of previous sexual intimacy. There is a consistent tendency for women to judge rape more seriously than men. Men who hold rape-supportive beliefs and adversarial attitudes toward women are more likely to be sexually aggressive. The attitudes supporting acquaintance rape need to be challenged vigorously to bring about social change.

7.36 Wyer, Robert S.; Galen V. Bodenhausen; and Theresa F. Gorman
1985 "Cognitive Mediators of Reactions to Rape." Journal of Personality and Social Psychology 48,2:324-338.

Purpose: To determine the effects of viewing aggression, intimacy, sexual exploitation of women, and sexually arousing images on reactions (applicability and judgment) to stranger and acquaintance and resisted and nonresisted rape.
Method: Thirty-five male and thirty-five female undergraduates gathered through volunteer sampling viewed slides portraying one of six situations: acts of aggression, negative outcomes of aggression, men and women in intimate, but not sexual acts, nonarousing images of women as sex objects, sexually arousing photographs of women, and women engaging in self-stimulation. Then, each subject read the testimony of a rape victim in which the perpetuator was either an acquaintance or a stranger and the victim either did or did not resist. Afterwards, the subjects completed a questionnaire in which they determined the responsibility of the victim, the harm done to her, the validity of the testimony, and the likelihood that the perpetrator should and

would be convicted.

Findings: A victim who did not resist was rated as more responsible for the rape especially if the perpetrator was an acquaintance. Men were more likely to state that the perpetrator should be convicted when the victim resisted regardless of their relationship. Women, however, stated that the perpetrator should be convicted when the victim resisted only if they were not acquaintances. Aggression-related slides. Viewing slides of aggression was related to increases in beliefs that the perpetrator should be convicted and that the victim was partly responsible. These effects become stronger when the perpetrator was not an acquaintance. Intimacy-related slides. Viewing slides of intimate relationships increased belief in the validity of the victim's testimony and extent of harm and decreased ratings of victim responsibility. Women as sex object slides. After viewing slides portraying women as sex objects, men increased their ratings of victim responsibility and decreased their beliefs in the validity of victim testimony. The effects were the opposite for women who viewed these slides. The effects of viewing the slides was reduced for both men and women when the perpetrator was an acquaintance and the victim did not resist.

8

ATTRIBUTION OF RESPONSIBILITY FOR ACQUAINTANCE RAPE

8.1 Abbey, Antonia
1987 "Perceptions of Personal Avoidability Versus Responsibility: How Do They Differ?" Basic and Applied Social Psychology 8,1&2:3-19.

Purpose: To examine and differentiate between attributions of self-blame and feelings of avoidance. Much of the self blame evidenced in personal accounts of rape may be seen as elements of how the person may avoid such behavior in the future. It is described by the author as a pilot study to generate future research.
Method: 24 rape victims were interviewed using a standardized format. The interview employed a combination of open- and closed-ended response items. Respondents were asked to assign responsibility to their attacker, society, chance, themselves, their behavior, and their character. Open-ended questions included asking them if they had asked themselves "why me?" and their own response to the question.
Findings: On the average, victims felt only slightly responsible for their experience. They were not likely to think that the way they behaved or their personality had anything to do with the attack. Those that did cited being out late alone, dressing up, or flirting with a co-worker as things that they might change. They did not perceive others as holding them very responsible. "Why Me" issues were addressed in terms of personal attribution for the most part, but also in terms of avoidance rather than self-blame.

67% of the victims felt that the attack was somehow avoidable. Overall, victims seemed to differentiate between responsibility for the attack and measures that could have been taken to avoid the attack.

8.2 Acock, Alan C. and Nancy K. Ireland
1983 "Attribution of Blame in Rape Cases: The Impact of Norm Violation, Gender and Sex Role Attitude." Sex Roles 9,2:179-193.

Purpose: The study measures the importance of the characteristics of the rape victim to those of the observer in the attribution of blame in rape cases.
Method: Undergraduate students were presented with two rape scenarios. In one, the victim is portrayed as a college student who is raped while walking home from the library at dusk and in the other the victim is portrayed as violating traditional sex role norms when she gives a man a ride to his car which had run out of gas. Subjects' sex role attitudes were measured as well as their perceptions of: seriousness of the crime, norm violation, respectability of the victim as a person, blame of the victim for the rape, blame of the rapist for the rape, and behavior intent of the victim and rapist.
Findings: The victim who behaved in a nontraditional way was blamed more for the assault and her rapist was blamed less. Subjects with traditional sexual role attitudes were likely to blame the victim more and rapist less in both rape situations. This research suggests the need to study both the characteristics of the victim and observer in the attribution process.

8.3 Bridges, Judith S. and Christine A. McGrail
1989 "Attributions of Responsibility for Date and Stranger Rape." Sex Roles 21,3/4: 273-286.

Purpose: The study examines attribution of responsibility for rape based on victim-perpetrator relationship.

Method: Undergraduate students, 122 female and 62 male, participated in a 3x2x2 factorial experimental design that varied victim-perpetrator relationship; occurrence of rape; and sex of the subject. After reading one of six scenarios, subjects responded to a series of scales that measured sex role expectations, rape supportive beliefs, and victim and perpetrator responsibility.
Findings: Subjects attributed more responsibility to the victim in the date rape scenario as opposed to the stranger rape scenario. The victim's disreputable qualities, her provocative behavior and/or appearance, and her failure to control the situation all contributed to subjects' attribution of blame. In comparison to females, males reported higher attributions to provocative victims, failure to control on the part of the victim, and perpetrator's excessive sex drive. Stranger rapists are seen as more responsible than date rapists. Similarly, the male who raped on a first date was seen as more responsible than one who raped in a steady dating relationship.

8.4 Calhoun, Karen S. and Ruth M. Townsley
1991 "Attributions of Responsibility for Acquaintance Rape." Pp. 57-70 in Acquaintance Rape: The Hidden Crime, edited by Andrea Parrot and Laurie Bechhofer. New York: John Wiley and Sons.

Purpose: To review the research on situations in which acquaintance rape assailants are not found blameworthy, but the victims are held responsible for the rape.
Method: Review of literature.
Findings: It is important to maintain distinctions among attributions of causes, responsibility, and blameworthiness. Research has shown that males tend to be more victim-blaming than females, and those holding traditional attitudes toward women or traditional sex-role attitudes are more likely to blame the victim. More research is needed on other potentially important variables such as victim characteristics and behavior, offender characteristics, observer characteristics, and situational variables.

8.5 Coller, Sarah A. and Patricia A. Resick
1987 "Women's Attributions of Responsibility for Date Rape: The Influence of Empathy and Sex-Role Stereotyping." Violence and Victims 2,2:115-125.

Purpose: The study examines the connections between sex role stereotyping, empathy with the victim, and attribution of blame in a date rape scenario.
Method: Seventy six female undergraduate students were presented with vignettes that manipulated the degree of victim empathy. They then responded to a questionnaire that measured their attribution of responsibility between the victim and offender. The Sexual Experiences Survey was used to determine the subjects' personal experiences with sexual assault.
Findings: High sex role stereotyping individuals blamed the victim more often than low sex role stereotyping women. Traditional women were also more likely to indicate that the victim led the offender on and thus saw the offender as less responsible for what happened. They also rated his action more justifiable. There was no significant effect for the victim-empathy score. Similarly, whether the subject had experienced an attempted or completed sexual assault did not affect the way she defined the situation, the degree of empathy for the victim, or the degree of blame she engaged in. Past sexual victimization also did not affect the woman's adherence to sex role stereotyping.

8.6 Fenstermaker, Sarah
1989 "Acquaintance Rape on Campus: Attributions of Responsibility and Crime." Pp. 257-271 in Violence in Dating Relationships, edited by Maureen Pirog-Good and Jan Stets. New York: Praeger.

Purpose: To measure the incidence of sexual coercion and analyze factors that influence interpretations of sexually coercive situations.
Method: A two-part questionnaire was mailed to a probability

sample of 15% of male and female undergraduate students. Only female responses are included in this article. Part one of the questionnaire presented students with an initial scenario where a male and female were studying together and through the course of the night, he forces her to have sexual intercourse despite her protests. Subjects were then presented with seven variations of the scenario. Location of date, type of date, level of intimacy, and past intimacy were varied. Subjects were asked to attribute responsibility to the man and woman, to decide whether a crime had been committed, and whether the female should report it to the police. Part two of the questionnaire asked students to indicate their experiences with specific types of sexually coercive behavior. Findings: 74% of the respondents had not experienced any sexual coercion in their dating relationships. Seven percent had experiences that could be classified as felony crimes. Of those who indicated that they had been sexually coerced, 56% had experienced coercion more than once. The degree of male responsibility varied across the vignettes. Male responsibility declined when the female voluntarily engaged in necking and petting prior to the unwanted sexual intercourse, when the male and the female had a history of prior intercourse, and when both the male and female were under the influence of alcohol. When there was at least initial consent by the female, the behavior was less likely to be labelled a crime. As ratings for male responsibility dropped, so did the sense that a crime had been committed.

8.7 Ferguson, Patricia A.; Dolores A. Duthie; and Richard G. Graf

1987 "Attribution of Responsibility to Rapist and Victim: the Influence of Victim's Attractiveness and Rape-Related Information." Journal of Interpersonal Violence 2,3:243-250.

Purpose: The study tests the hypothesis that giving information about the motives of rape will influence observers' attribution of responsibility to a rape victim.

Method: Forty male undergraduate students were randomly assigned to one of four conditions in a 2x2 factorial design. Subjects were presented with one of two photographs, one attractive and the other unattractive, of a rape victim. Subjects were then presented with one of two sets of information. One contained information taken from an article about sexual aggression and the other contained information on nutrition taken from a textbook. They were then presented with a rape scenario depicting the victim whose photo they had viewed. Finally, subjects were asked to assess both victim and perpetrator responsibility for the rape.
Findings: The data suggest that giving subjects objective information creates a bias against unattractive victims. Subjects who received information on nutrition, the uniformed condition, attributed greater blame to the rapist of the attractive victim and less blame to the rapist of the unattractive victim. There were no differences in the amount of blame directed at the rapist in the informed condition. However, when comparing informed and uninformed subjects who viewed an unattractive victim, informed subjects gave the rapist more blame than uninformed subjects. Giving specific information on sexual aggression does not guarantee that subjects will hold rapists responsible. There were several informed subjects who attributed responsibility to the victim.

8.8 Goodchilds, J.D.; G.L. Zellman; P.B. Johnson; and R. Giarusso

1988 "Adolescents and Their Perceptions of Sexual Interactions." Pp. 245-279 in Sexual Assault, Volume II, edited by A.W. Burgess. New York: Garland.

Purpose: To examine the following issues: 1) adolescent perceptions of responsibility for dating outcomes, 2) adolescents cues and signals concerning sexuality, 3) expectations for dating relationships, and 4) application of the label "rape" to nonconsensual sex between acquaintances.

Method: The sample consisted of 432 Los Angeles adolescents, one-half of each sex and one-third of each major ethnic group (black, white, hispanic). Subjects evaluated vignettes and attributed levels of responsibility to each person involved. These varied by setting, force used, and relationship. Cues and signals were measured by subjects response to a list of things that "a guy and a girl might do". They rated these as to whether the situation was one where the male or female might want to have sex. Expectations were evaluated by subject descriptions of dating qualities. They also answered a set of questions about a dates clothing. The use of the label "rape" was evaluated by using a series of vignettes, and having subjects define each.
Findings: Males and females apportioned responsibility equally. Initiators were seen as more responsible, regardless of outcome. Overall, they tended to support a male-dominated sexual scenario, men being most responsible whether sex was an outcome or not. Cuing and signaling generally supported the view that males tend to attribute greater sexuality to more situations. Both males and females felt that males were more interested in sex. Dating expectations fell along similar lines, each gender attributing more sexual content to men. Both males and females believed that actors in the situations would disagree about the meaning of the cues employed. No main effects by sex were shown in the definition of rape. Rape was more likely to be defined by a woman's objections rather than a man's. They were most likely to define rape where the couple had just met and the male made a clear use of force, least likely where a minimum of force was used in a dating relationship.

8.9 Jacobson, Marsha B. and Paula M. Popovich
1983 "Victim Attractiveness and Perceptions of Responsibility in an Ambiguous Rape Case." Psychology of Women Quarterly 8,1:100-104.

Purpose: The study examines the extent to which a rape victim's attractiveness affects the attribution of responsibility in an ambiguous rape scenario.

Method: Undergraduate students participated in a 2x2x2 factorial design experiment where victim attractiveness, defendant attractiveness, and sex of subject were varied. Subjects read a scenario of 2 college students who worked on a project together. Minimal details of the rape were presented so it was unclear whether a rape took place or not. They were asked their perceptions of the scenario and shown pictures of the offender and victim.

Findings: Attractive victims were perceived as more careless, responsible and provocative than the unattractive victim. The offender was perceived as more likely to want to rape an attractive woman as compared to an unattractive one. The Findings indicate a double standard for attractive victims and offenders. Although attractive victims were seen as more responsible for a rape, subjects recommended shorter prison sentences for attractive defendants.

8.10 Jenkins, Megan and Faye Dambrot

1987 "The Attribution of Date Rape: Observer's Attitudes and Sexual Experiences and The Dating Situation." Journal of Applied Social Psychology 17,10:875-895.

Purpose: The study examines the relationship between subjects' experiences with sexual victimization/aggression, their acceptance of rape myths, and situational factors of rape attribution.

Method: Undergraduate students, 323 female and 332 males, read a date rape scenario. Three scenarios were randomly assigned to students and were exactly the same except for who paid for the date and how the date was planned. Subjects were asked to rate how planned the meeting between the man and woman was and the amount of money that the man spent on the woman. Sexual Experiences were measured with the Sexual Experiences Survey and rape myth acceptance was measured with a revision of Burt's 7 point scale.

Findings: Compared to women, men showed a higher acceptance of rape myths, were less likely to view forced intercourse as rape, and were more likely to see the rape victim as desiring sexual intercourse. Women's individual experiences of sexual victimization did not affect their rape attributions but men's experiences of sexual aggression did. Sexually assaultive males had the highest agreement that the victim wanted intercourse and lowest agreement that rape had occurred in scenario and that the assailant had used violence. Women, however, were less likely to view forced sexual intercourse as rape in the planned date where the man paid. Situational factors did not affect men's attributions.

8.11 Richardson, Deborah and Campbell, Jennifer L.
1982 "Alcohol and Rape: The Effect of Alcohol on Attributions of Blame for Rape." Personality and Social Psychology Bulletin 8,3:468-476.

Purpose: The goal of this study was to determine whether intoxication on the part of a rape victim and/or rape perpetrator influences observer's attributions about blame.
Method: A vignette survey was read by 187 undergraduates. Intoxication of victim and offender were manipulated in the vignettes. Subjects were then asked to assign percentages of blame to the victim, to the offender, and to the situation in which the rape occurred. They were also asked to rate the responsibility of the victim and of the offender; to rate the victim and offender on a series of personality traits; to estimate the likelihood of prosecution and conviction; to describe how the police would be likely to respond, and how they should respond.
Findings: Victim intoxication was associated with greater victim responsibility and with perceptions of the victim as less moral, more aggressive, less likeable, and less easy to identify with. Conversely, offender intoxication was associated with less offender blame and less offender responsibility. Male subjects were more likely than females to believe that the case would go to court and that the offender would be convicted, and males also recommended longer prison sentences. Male subjects thought that a conviction was most likely when both the victim and the offender were sober, while female subjects thought a conviction most likely when the

offender was drunk and the victim was sober.

8.12 Shotland, Lance R. and Lynne Goodstein
1983 "Just Because She Doesn't Want to Doesn't Mean It's Rape: An Experimentally Based Causal Model of the Perception of Rape in a Dating Situation." Social Psychology Quarterly 46,3:220-232.

Purpose: The goal of the study was to determine how various characteristics of a date rape scenario, and attitudes of observers, influence observers' attributions about date rape.
Method: 287 undergraduates were asked to read a date rape vignette in which the following dimensions were manipulated: onset of victim's protest, type of protest, and force used by offender. After reading the vignette, subjects rendered a number of judgments: how much was the victim responsible/at fault for the assault, how much did the victim really want to have sex, how violent was the man, and did the event constitute rape. Three scales created by Helmreich and Spence were administered to measure subjects' gender identification: the M (masculinity) scale, the F (femiminity) scale, and the MF (androgyny) scale. Helmreich and Spence's Attitudes Towards Women scale was also administered to assess subjects' sex-role attitudes.
Findings: The victim was perceived as wanting to have sex more when her protest occurred later, when the man used greater force, and among subjects with traditional sex-role attitudes. The victim was blamed more when the man used little force, when her protest occurred later in the date, and among subjects with traditional sex-role attitudes and higher scores on the masculinity scale. Subjects were more likely to describe the offender as violent when the victim used physical and verbal protest strategics, and when her protest began earlier in the date. The man was also seen as more violent among subjects with egalitarian sex-role attitudes and among those scoring higher on the masculinity scale. The situation was more likely to be described as rape when both physical and verbal protest strategies were used, when the protest began earlier in the date, and among subjects with egalitarian sex-

role attitudes and those scoring higher on the masculinity scale. Path models of rape attribution were also performed. The authors suggest that verbal protest may not be enough to convince observers that a rape occurred; some evidence of the woman's unwillingness to have sex, such as man's force or woman's physical protest, may be necessary.

8.13 Tetreault, Patricia A. and Mark A. Barnett
1987 "Reactions to Stranger and Acquaintance Rape." Psychology of Women Quarterly, 11:353-358.

Purpose: The authors examined gender differences in reactions to rape based upon whether the offender was a stranger or an acquaintance.
Method: 80 male and female undergraduates read one of two vignettes depicting a rape scenario. In one vignette, the assailant was an acquaintance of the victim; in the other, he was a stranger. Subjects then viewed a videotape of a therapy session in which the victim (an actress) described her reactions to the rape. Subjects were asked to rate the victim's responsibility, whether a rape had occurred, the severity of the assault, and their attitudes towards the victim.
Findings: Female subjects were more likely to believe that a rape actually occurred, that the woman was less responsible, and that the assault was more serious, when the assailant was a stranger. The exact reverse reaction was noted among men. Female subjects found the rape victim more likable than male subjects did, and male subjects found the victim much less likable when the rape was committed by a stranger.

8.14 Tieger, Todd
1981 "Self-rated Likelihood of Raping and the Social Perception of Rape." Journal of Research in Personality 15:147-158.

Purpose: This study explored the relationship between sex, sex-role tendencies, attitudes about rape, and self-rated proclivity to rape (men only).

Method: 392 undergraduates read a rape vignette in which only the photograph of the victim (attractive vs unattractive) was manipulated. Subjects then responded to items regarding the victim's believability, victim precipitation, severity of the assault, rapist's motivation for the crime, and victim's enjoyment of the rape. Men were also asked how likely it was that they themselves would commit rape if they knew they wouldn't get caught. All subjects completed the Bem Sex Role Inventory (BSRI).

Findings: Factor analysis was performed on the dependent variables, yielding seven factors. Males tended to blame the nonattractive victim more than females. The nonattractive victim was perceived as more responsible than the attractive victim, especially by males. Subjects with more feminine BSRI scores were most likely to believe the victim, and to rate the crime as very severe. Males blamed the victim for failing to resist more than females, especially when the victim was attractive. Males were more likely than females to view the rapist's motivation as sexual. Almost one-third of male subjects reported that they might commit rape if they knew they wouldn't get caught. A high likelihood of raping was associated with victim blaming, with a view of the crime as not very serious, with a view of the rapist as sexually motivated and psychologically normal, and with a higher perceived attractiveness of the victim. The authors suggest that a high self-reported likelihood of raping is associated with a set of disinhibitory beliefs about rape.

9

LEGAL ISSUES

9.1 Bessmer, Sue
1984 The Laws of Rape. New York: Praeger.

Purpose: The objective of this research is to examine how socio-cultural attitudes, values, and mores regarding women and sexuality may influence the content of rape laws.
Method: 200 appellate court decisions were analyzed.
Findings: Rape laws often serve to protect social values and norms. In particular, rape threatens the institution of marriage by (1) violating the norm of premarital chastity, (2) hurting a woman's chances of marrying, or (3) interfering with an existing marital relationship. Because rape laws are geared to preserving the system of monogamous marriage, they tend to do a better job of protecting future and present participants in that system. Thus, rape laws often divide alleged victims into "worthy" and "unworthy" categories based upon the victim's age, sexual history, marital status, lifestyle, "morality," and so on. Gender inequality and power relations also determine the extent to which rape is seen as a crime, and the treatment of victims by the legal system and society in general.

9.2 Bohmer, Carol
1991 "Acquaintance Rape and the Law." Pp 317-34 in Acquaintance Rape: The Hidden Crime, edited by Andrea Parrot and Laurie Bechhofer. New York:

John Wiley and Sons.

Purpose: To examine laws concerning rape and changes in laws in recent years. Particular reference is made to how the law affects how acquaintance rape is dealt with by the legal system.
Method: Review of literature and case law.
Findings: The issue of consent and proof of nonconsent have made it particularly difficult to prosecute rape cases, especially acquaintance rape, which is less likely to involve a weapon. Rape laws have been reformed to deal with the difficulty of demonstrating lack of consent, but the reforms have not had the dramatic effect hoped for by those advocating the reforms. The reforms have had little effect on the likelihood of conviction, and efforts to promote more reforms have faltered. The way the law deals with acquaintance rape is intimately linked to attitudes toward appropriate sexual behavior, and until these change, it is unlikely that the law will be more responsive to the crime of acquaintance rape.

9.3 Bohmer, Carol and Andrea Parrot
1993 Sexual Assault on Campus: The Problem and the Solution. N.Y.: Lexington Books.

Purpose: To describe how sexual assault, date and acquaintance rape cases are being handled by college campuses and to make recommendations about how these cases should be handled. The book is intended for victims, those working with victims, and college administrators.
Method: This is primarily an advice book more than a reporting of empirical research. Case studies of sexual assault are used to demonstrate the major points made, but these are illustrative rather than research results per se. There is some review of the scholarly literature as well, although this is not a systematic literature review.
Findings: Since this is primarily intended to advise victims and college administrators, there are not "findings" as there are for reports of empirical research. The "findings" consist primarily of

recommendations for the handing of assault cases. For instance, in a "checklist for victims and their parents," the authors advise that if a victim feels the college is not handling the case properly, she should try to deal with the college directly; she might consider hiring a lawyer, and if she does, one should be selected carefully; she should tell the lawyer everything; she should use all the support available; etc. A similar checklist is provided for colleges to "avoid lawsuits." It includes: check the campus for safety problems; inform students about safety policies; pay careful attention to due process in the code of conduct; include the rights of victims in the code of conduct; consult with the college attorney in cases of threatened suits; etc. This is an excellent resource for those dealing with acquaintance rape on campuses.

9.4 Estrich, Susan
1987 Real Rape: How the Legal System Victimizes Women Who Say No. Cambridge: Harvard University Press.

Purpose: To review and analyze the way law addresses "simple rape"--rape in which a single defendant rapes someone he knows without using or threatening to use a weapon. The book is an attempt to contribute to efforts to change the law and the treatment of simple rape (frequently acquaintance rape) by the legal system.
Method: Review of laws and law cases dealing with simple rape. This is the first comprehensive review of such laws to be published.
Findings: Cases of simple rape have traditionally been treated very differently by the law than cases of "aggravated rape." Aggravated rape is defined as rape by a stranger who uses violence or threatens to do so. The analysis demonstrates that in cases of simple rape, distrust of the woman victim was an important part of the definition of the crime, and the rules of proof were different than those for aggravated rape. Despite reforms in the 1970s and 1980s, the review of cases indicates that the successful prosecution of rape cases still required the demonstration that the perpetrator used force to overpower the

victim. The right of male sexual access in certain relationships continued to be protected by the law and its application to the prosecution of simple rape cases. Estrich makes suggestions about further reforms to produce laws that signal that simple rape is real rape.

9.5 Feild, Hubert S. and Leigh B. Bienen
1980 Jurors and Rape: A Study in Psychology and Law. Lexington, MA: Lexington Books.

Purpose: This book addresses legal issues relevant to cases of rape.
Method: The first half of the book describes the results of a vignette survey which was administered to 1448 adults, including smaller subsamples of police officers, female rape crisis counselors, and convicted rapists. Respondents were presented with a fictional rape case file including photographs of the mock victim and defendant, mock transcripts of testimony, and a mock police report describing the circumstances of the assault. Respondents also completed the Attitudes Toward Rape and the Attitudes Towards Women scales, along with a rape knowledge test. They were then asked to render a verdict, to describe the certainty of their verdict, and to assign a prison sentence (if applicable.)
Findings: Among white respondents, variables associated with harsher sentencing included a white victim, a black defendant, strong corroborating evidence, and a lack of victim precipitation (i.e., the defendant breaking into the victim's apartment versus being invited in). Among black respondents, however, only the strength of the evidence was significantly related to sentencing decisions. Characteristics of respondents which were associated with harsher sentencing included: being older (whites only), having less education, and having not previously served on a jury (blacks only). Attitudes associated with less harsh sentencing included the beliefs that women are responsible for preventing rape, that rape is motivated by sexual desire (blacks only), that some women provoke rape (whites only), and that rapists are

basically normal men (whites only). A number of two- and three-way interaction effects are also reported.

The second half of the book is devoted to a discussion of recent reform laws regarding rape. This section also contains an extensive review of the rape laws of each state.

9.6 LaFree, Gary
1989 Rape and Criminal Justice: The Social Construction of Sexual Assault. Belmont, CA: Wadsworth.

Purpose: To discuss theoretical perspectives on sexual assault and recent developments in criminology, and to present empirical tests of some of the theoretical predictions presented. The guiding theoretical view of the work is that crime is not an objective phenomenon inherent in certain types of behavior, but that it is socially constructed through interaction.
Method: The empirical aspect of the work is an attempt to test conflict theory and labelling theory about how rape is dealt with by the criminal justice system. LaFree studies the processing of rape at several points in the criminal justice system: the police, the courts, and juries. The data are from reported rape cases in Indianapolis in the 1970s. The data come from police and court records and from observations of court proceedings and interviews with jurors.
Findings: There is partial support for the labelling perspective in the police data. Victim nonconformity, race composition, and number of offenders were significant predictors of police decisions. Other variables that are more clearly objective characteristics of the crime are also important; these include type of offense, presence of a weapon, and seriousness of the offense. The data on courts and juror evaluations provide a similar picture. The findings are based on an analysis of reported rapes, so both stranger and acquaintance rapes are included in the analysis. This work is most relevant to acquaintance rape in its examination of the relationship between victim and offender, and the impact of this relationship on the processing of cases by the criminal justice

system.

9.7 Lyons, Arthur W. and Regina, Joanne
1986 "Mock Jurors' Behavior as a Function of Sex and Exposure to an Educational Videotape About Jury Duty." Psychological Reports 58:599-604.

Purpose: The purpose of this research was to ascertain the effects of an educational videotape about jury duty on mock jurors' assignment of verdicts and sentencing in a mock rape trial.
Method: 86 undergraduates volunteered as jurors in a mock rape trial. The experimental group (N not given) was shown an educational video about jury duty while the control group viewed a video on an unrelated topic. Following the videos, subjects read a rape scenario and assigned a verdict to the case. If a guilty verdict was reached, subjects also recommended a sentence. (NOTE: While the authors fail to indicate whether this was an acquaintance rape scenario, the key issue in the case was consent.)

Findings: Subjects in the experimental group were less likely than control subjects to convict the defendant, but when they did, they imposed longer sentences. Women in both groups were more likely than men to convict. Men in the experimental group imposed much longer sentences than any other group. The authors suggest that the tape resulted in jurors making more careful decisions, which led to harsher sentencing, especially for men.

9.8 Spohn, Cassia and Julie Horney
1992 Rape Law Reform: A Grassroots Revolution and Its Impact. New York: Plenum Press.

Purpose: The purpose of this research was to evaluate the impact of a variety of rape law reforms in six major cities in the United States. These specific reforms were as follows: definitional changes (e.g., the addition of lesser charges such as sexual battery); elimination of corroborating evidence and proof-of-

resistance requirements; and various rape shield reforms (e.g. limiting the amount of irrelevant evidence regarding victims' sexual histories).
Method: The analysis included all cases of rape reported in these six cities over a fifteen-year period (1970-85), resulting in a sample of over 22,000 cases.
Findings: The overall findings of the evaluation indicate that the reforms were successful at reducing the amount of irrelevant evidence regarding victims' prior sexual histories; however, these reforms had little impact on the admissibility of evidence regarding prior sexual contact between the victim and the defendant. The reforms also had little impact on the importance of corroborating evidence and proof of victim resistance for obtaining convictions. Finally, the reforms were not associated with increases in convictions, and were associated with only limited increases in reporting by victims and in the likelihood of indictment of alleged offenders. Specific findings regarding the nature, implementation, and impact of each type of reform are also presented.

9.9 Temkin, Jennifer
1986 "Women, Rape and Law Reform." Pp. 16-39 in Rape, edited by Sylvana Tomaselli and Roy Porter. Oxford: Basil Blackwell.

Purpose: To analyze the treatment of rape in the criminal justice system and rape laws in Michigan, Canada, and England.
Method: Integrative review of literature.
Findings: Discusses the Women Against Rape (WAR) study in England that found that almost all of the rape cases reported by women were committed by acquaintances. None of these cases were reported to the police. Perceptions of police attitudes as unsympathetic and unbelieving were believed to be the cause of the lack of reporting. In the analysis of rape law reform in Michigan, Canada, and England in the 1970's and 1980's, the extent to which the laws have included marital rape as a crime is discussed.

10

CAMPUS RAPE

Many of the studies of campus rape are included elsewhere in the bibliography. As indicated in Chapter 1, the vast majority of the studies of incidence of date and acquaintance has been carried out on college campuses. These studies are included in Chapter 2 on Incidence of Acquaintance Rape. To help identify campus studies, a listing of all studies with a campus sample is given at the end of this chapter.

10.1 Lott, Bernice; Mary Ellen Reilly; and Dale R. Howard
1982 "Sexual Assault and Harassment: A Campus Community Case Study." Signs: Journal of Women in Culture and Society 8,2:297-319.

Purpose: Following a public debate about acts of sexual aggression on the University of Rhode Island Campus, a committee was formed to investigate what students, faculty and staff thought about the campus situation, what experience they had had with sexual assault and harassment, and their attitudes about sexual aggression.
Method: Researchers drew a random sample of 1,954 students, faculty and staff which was representative of the actual proportions of these groups in the campus population. All subjects were mailed a 30-minute questionnaire along with a consent form for a subsequent in-person interview. 927 usable questionnaires were

returned, and 61 of these subjects participated in an in-person interview.

Findings: In the questionnaires, 13% of the sample reported knowing at least one person (other than themselves) who had experienced sexual assault on-campus, and about 6% reported that they themselves had been sexually assaulted on-campus. The majority of all of these assaults took place in or near a dormitory or other campus residence. 29% of the women and 5% of the men reported that they had been sexually assaulted at some point in their lives somewhere off-campus. Among males, faculty and administrators were most likely to indicate that they had been sexually assaulted; no status differences were noted for women. In the on-campus sexual assaults 31% of the victims reported that the perpetrators were strangers, vs 39% in the off-campus incidents; however, rapes by strangers were more likely to be reported to police. Smaller proportions of subjects reported being sexually harassed or intimidated, and even fewer reported engaging in such intimidation themselves. 9% of women reported leaving a job at least once due to sexual harassment, but very few students reported dropping a class for this reason. Males and younger subjects were more tolerant of sexual harassment.

In the interviews, many subjects, especially younger women, expressed the belief that sexual aggression is simply a fact of life. Many felt that alcohol is a major factor in most sexual assaults. Most believed that it is up to women to avoid sexual assault. Most were pessimistic about the probability of a rapist being convicted. Some felt that the issue of sexual aggression on campus had been exaggerated.

10.2 Martin, Patricia Yancey and Robert A. Hummer
1989 "Fraternities and Rape on Campus." Gender & Society 3,4:457-473.

Purpose: To analyze college fraternities focusing on the dynamics related to the social construction of fraternity life and the processes that work to make fraternities an abusive social context for women.

Method: The analysis began with a case study of an alleged gang rape at a fraternity at Florida State University. The data were gathered through content analysis at over 100 newspaper articles on the case, open-ended interviews of Greek and non-Greek university students (N=20), university administrators (N=8), Greek organization advisors (N=6), judges, defense attorneys, victim advocates, and state prosecutors. Grounded theory was used to analyze the data.
Findings: Fraternities serve as physical and sociocultural context that result in sexual coercion of women. As a result of the form of the organization, the types of members, the practices of members, and the general absence of university and community involvement, fraternities are sights of many date rapes. Specific masculine qualities including competition, dominance, absence and condemnation of feminine traits, willingness to consume alcohol, and sexual prowess are valued and necessary in members. These values contribute to the sexual coercion of women. Practices of fraternity members further contribute to the creation of fraternity atmosphere which leads to date rape: (1) Extensive emphasis on loyalty, group protection, and secrecy results in members protection of the fraternity over personal ethics or the law, (2) History of violence and physical force is apparent in hazing practices, fighting, vandalism, and rape, (3) Alcohol use is a necessary and normative practice of fraternity members and is commonly used both individually and collectively to coerce women into having sex, and (4) Competition and intrafraternity rivalries is particularly intense over women. Women are commodified by the fraternity to be used as bait to recruit new members, to host and serve at parties and to be used as sexual prey. The "Little Sister" program exemplifies the commodification of women by fraternities, and promotes a gender hierarchy on campus.

10.3 Schwartz, Martin D.
1991 "Humanist Sociology and Date Rape on the College Campus." Humanity and Society 15,3:304-316.

Purpose: The study reviews past research on the incidence of acquaintance rape on campus and the social factors that make campus a fertile ground for such violence. The author suggests that sociologists, and faculty in general, have a unique opportunity of doing something about the problem in their community rather than just theorizing about it.
Method: Literature review
Findings: The incidence of acquaintance rape on campus has been well documented over the past 30 years ranging from Kanin in 1957 to Koss et al. in 1987. The author suggests that there are particular social structural factors in American society and on college campuses that encourage men to rape women. Fraternities, in particular, provide a social structure as well as a socialization process that encourages men to devalue women. Studies have supported the hypothesis that fraternity men are more likely to be involved in gang rape on campus. Individually, fraternity men can be distinguished from other men on campus as being more likely to engage in a higher frequency of sexually coercive acts toward women. Colleges and universities are implementing temporary steps to end acquaintance rape on campus. The most common step is to tell students to stop committing felony crimes, but the institutions fail to take steps to provide a safer environment on campus. Things that could be done to ensure safety include the provision of services for victims; developing clear policies against acquaintance rape and disciplinary proceedings; educating students in general about rape and men specifically on issues of male violence in the context of patriarchy.

Additional studies on campus rape: 2.2, 2.3, 2.5, 2.9, 2.11-18, 2.20-21, 2.23-24, 2.26-29, 2.31, 2.33-36, 3.2-4, 3.6, 3.8, 3.11, 3.12, 3.16, 4.1, 4.2, 4.4-7, 5.1, 5.4-8, 5.10-12, 5.14, 5.18, 5.19, 5.21, 7.1, 7.3, 7.7, 7.9, 7.11-16, 7.19-25, 7.27-29, 7.31-33, 7.36, 8.2, 8.3, 8.7, 8.9, 8.10, 8.12, 8.13, 9.7, 10.1, 10.3, 12.3, 12.4, 13.8, 13.12, 14.3-8, 14.10

11

MARITAL RAPE

11.1 Finkelhor, David and Kersti Yllo
1985 License to Rape: Sexual Abuse of Wives. New York: Holt, Rinehart and Winston.

Purpose: The authors' purpose was to describe the incidence, form, nature and consequences of rape by a spouse.
Method: This book is based on a survey of 323 Boston-area women, on in-depth interviews with 50 marital rape victims, and a literature review.
Findings: In the survey, women were asked about their experience with marital rape and other kinds of sexual assault. The authors found that 10% of the sample reported a rape or attempted rape committed by their husband, a percentage which exceeded other forms of sexual assault reported by the sample. Characteristics of women which were associated with marital rape in this sample included being divorced or separated, coming from a lower socio-economic background, being Protestant or atheist, being under 30 or over 50, and having a history of childhood sexual abuse.

The in-depth interviews with marital rape survivors, an attitude survey of college students, and the sexual assault literature and other media provide the basis for the remaining chapters. Chapters 2 through 7 review the nature, forms, and impact of marital rape, including characteristics of husbands who rape their wives. It is emphasized that, for many marital rape victims, nonsexual battering is also a feature of the relationship. Chapters 8 and 9 address legal and social issues hampering the successful prosecution of marital rape. Chapter 10 considers possible prevention strategies.

11.2 Frieze, Irene
1983 "Investigating the Causes and Consequences of Marital Rape." Signs: Journal of Women in Culture and Society 8:532-553.

Purpose: To investigate the frequency, causes of, and reactions to marital rape.
Method: 137 women were interviewed using structured interviews. Each woman was asked if sex between her husband and her was ever unpleasant, if there was violence in her marriage, and if she had ever been raped by her husband.
Findings: The women were most likely to report being sexually pressured or being forced to have sex than to report that they had been raped or forced to perform repugnant acts. Three percent of the women reported marital rape. However, many of the women who experienced acts that meet the legal definitions of rape did not define the acts as rape. About 10 percent reported other forms of sexual force. Battered women reported the highest rates of all types of sexual assaults, while rape in nonviolent marriages was relatively rare. When asked why they believed they were raped, most (78%) believed that there husbands assaulted them in order to prove their manhood. Alcohol (14%) and frustration and outside events were also common reasons given. All women placed the responsibility for the rape on their husbands. When considering the variables that differentiate victims of marital rape from other women, the presence of violence appeared to be the strongest differentiator. The more violent the husband, the more likely he was to rape his wife. Analysis was then performed to compare battered women who had been raped and those who had not. The battered women who had been raped tended to have children, never have been employed, have little education and therefore, had many barriers to leaving the marriage.

Furthermore, the battered women who had been raped had more negative sexual relations with their husbands, had more violent husbands, and were significantly more likely to have been raped by someone other than their husband. There were no significant differences in experience of sexual molestation as a child. When considering reactions to marital rape, most women felt anger and other negative emotions. Battered women who had been raped were more likely to seek help than women, including battered women, who had not been raped. Ninety-six percent of battered women who had been raped attempted to leave their husbands and ninety-four percent sought psychological help. However, the women reported that seeking help was not easy and experienced various forms of hesitation.

11.3 Russell, Diana E. H.
1990 Rape in Marriage, Second Edition. Indianapolis: Indiana University.

Purpose: The goal of this research is to present a legal, social and interpersonal review of the crime of marital rape.
Method: 930 women over age 18 living in the San Francisco area were located through a telephone directory and then interviewed in their homes. The author supplements the findings of this study with information from legal sources, social science research, popular culture, and recent marital rape trials.
Findings: Of the women in the sample who had ever been married, 14% reported being raped by a husband or ex-husband. More women had been raped by husbands or ex-husbands than by any other single category of assailant; this proportion increased greatly when the number of attacks was controlled for. Marital rape was likely to be accompanied by beating. 84% of the husband-rapists used physical force to obtain compliance, 13% used a gun, 35% verbally threatened the victim with physical harm, and 15% threatened some non-physical consequence. About one-third of the victims had been raped once by a husband, and one-third over 20 times. 11% of victims spontaneously reported some injury during the interview. 21% of the victim-assailant

dyads were still married. Husbands' social class was unrelated to their propensity to rape, but husband-rapists were more likely to be between the ages of 21 and 30 and to be Caucasian. Being a victim of marital rape was significantly correlated with a number of other forms of sexual abuse, including non-marital rape and childhood sexual abuse; however, only 2 victims reported being raped by more than one husband. As was the case for husband-rapists, there were no social class differences between victims and non-victims, nor were there differences in wives' traditionality. However, Black wives were slightly more likely to report rape by a husband. Wife rape, in contrast to other forms of sexual abuse, appears to be among the most upsetting and having the most long-term negative effects. Overall, 19% of the wives who experienced marital violence reported it to the police; outcomes of these reports are discussed at some length.

Marital rape is conceptualized as one end of a continuum of sexual relations between husband and wife. The questions of why men rape their wives and ex-wives, the role of alcohol/drugs, and why raped wives stay in the marriage, are discussed in the context of theory and research from other sources. Torture and murder of wives, as well as a cross-national overview of wife rape, are also covered. Appendixes which describe recent marital rape trials and marital rape laws in the U.S. are included. Anecdotal evidence from the interviews is provided throughout.

11.4 Russell, Diana E.H.
1991 "Wife Rape." Pp. 129-139 in Acquaintance Rape: The Hidden Crime. New York: John Wiley and Sons.

Purpose: To review the history of wife rape and the law and to review the current status of marital rape in the legal system in the U.S.
Method: Review of laws and literature.
Findings: This chapter is adapted from Chapter 2 of Russell's book Rape in Marriage. See that entry for the details of her findings.

11.5 Yllo, Kersti and David Finkelhor
1985 "Marital Rape." Pp. 146-155 in Rape and Sexual Assault: A Research Handbook, edited by Ann Wolbert Burgess. New York: Garland.

Purpose: To review the first five years of research on marital rape in order to develop a definition, to examine the prevalence, the nature, effects, and legal issues associated with marital rape.
Method: Integrative review of literature
Findings: Rape in marriage has been defined in a variety of ways but can generally be defined similarly to other kinds of rape, however, it is the husband who forces his wife to have sex without her consent. The studies consistently reveal that marital rape is so widespread that is appears to be the most common form of rape. Findings reveal that between 3 and 14 percent of wives have been raped by their husbands. Battered wives report much higher rates of rape. The different types of marital rape which have been developed by researchers are presented and discussed. Contrary to popular belief, women who are raped by their husbands endure trauma as severe if not more than women who are raped by strangers. Lack of trust in and negative attitudes towards men, feelings of powerlessness, low self-esteem, and self blame are some of the consequences of marital rape for women. These effects are intensified as the marital rapes continue. The criminal justice system in the United States has reinforced the fact that the marriage license is essentially a raping license. Laws make prosecution of marital rape impossible and reinforce the assumption that marriage implies unquestionable consent by wives to all sexual advances by husbands. There is still a need for theoretical work, causal analysis, and research on husbands who rape.

12

GANG RAPE

12.1 Chancer, Lynn S.
1987 "New Bedford, Massachusetts, March 6, 1983-March 22, 1984: The Before and After of a Group Rape." Gender & Society 1:239-260.

Purpose: To examine the victim blaming reactions of a community following a publicized group rape legal case.
Method: Integrative use of mainstream news reports
Findings: The town, group rape incident, media reports, community responses to the media and the trial, and media's effect on community reactions are described. At first the predominantly Portuguese community of New Bedford was shocked and upset by the rape. However, soon attitudes of both men and women changed to great hostility and blaming of the victim and sympathy for the rapists. It is concluded that these attitudes were in reaction to what was perceived as a "victim-precipitated" rape. The extreme ethnic and sexual prejudice related to this case made it unique. The community was outraged at the media's portrayal of their ethnic group and blamed the rape victim for the prejudice, unwelcome media attention, and for the rape itself. The author concludes that this example adds support to theories of rape and reveals the need for more extensive feminist community organizations, including preexisting rape crisis centers.

12.2 Geis, Gilbert
1971 "Group Sexual Assault." Medical Aspects of Human Sexuality 5:101-13.

Purpose: To discuss the characteristics of group sexual assault and the perpetrators involved in the assaults.
Method: Integrative review of literature and case studies.
Findings: Rapes committed by a group of men involves established patterns of collective behavior. One of the men is generally the leader and plans the assault and is the first to rape the victim. The men involved in the assault are concerned with maintaining their images among the others. Victim blaming often accompanies group rape and the potential of ambivalence in victim's behavior is discussed. Statistics on group rapes are limited due to lack of research. One study that looked at group rapes found that 43 percent of rapes include more than one perpetrator and that 71 percent of perpetrators reported being involved in group rapes. Characteristics of group rapists include: youth, the use of alcohol, and past criminal records. Using past research, a model of the dynamics of group rape is developed.

12.3 O'Sullivan, Chris S.
1991 "Gang Rape on Campus." Pp. 140-56 in Acquaintance Rape: The Hidden Crime, edited by Andrea Parrot and Laurie Bechhofer. New York: John Wiley and Sons.

Purpose: To review the research on gang rape on college campuses. Questions addressed include what gang rape is, how often it occurs, who the perpetrators and victims are, and why it occurs.
Method: Review of literature.
Findings: Gang rape is defined as a group of men--three or more--having sex with a woman when her participation is involuntary. It is argued that gang rapes on college campuses are normative; they follow from conventional sex roles. Campus gang rapes are almost always acquaintance rapes that occur during or after parties.

Good data on the incidence of gang rapes are not available, but extrapolations from the rape literature and media reports indicate that it does occur. The most common age for perpetrators and victims is 20-24 years old. Cohesive groups such as fraternities and athletic teams are more likely to be involved in gang rapes. The normative factors that contribute to gang rape include attitudes toward women and women's sexuality, and men's attitudes toward their own sexuality. Prevention efforts need to include the problem of group norms and group pressure as well as individual attitude change.

12.4 Sanday, Peggy Reeves
1990 Fraternity Gang Rape: Sex, Brotherhood, and Privilege on Campus. New York: New York University Press.

Purpose: To analyze the cultural context that supports gang rape on college campuses.
Method: Sanday is an anthropologist, and she uses anthropological field methods to study gang rape. Specifically, she bases her analysis on in-depth interviews and field notes from several case studies of fraternity gang rape. The analysis is qualitative and focuses on the cultural norms and accompanying discourse that encourage gang rape, or "pulling train."
Findings: Gang rape is a form of sexual aggression that is defined as "normal" and expected by some men and women on college campuses. It is a means by which some fraternities display masculinity and indoctrinate new members to acceptable masculine power roles. It is rationalized by a comprehensive ideology of male dominance and privilege. Some of the cases studied indicate that the university response is too often to ignore or cover up the incidence of gang rape, a response which further promotes sexual aggression. Fraternity rituals such as initiation serve to reproduce a misogynist ideology that perpetuates sexual abuse. Sanday is careful to point out that she is not describing all fraternities on all college campuses; however, gang rapes such as those she describes "appear to be part of a widespread sexual pattern on college

campuses." Universities need to take careful, deliberate, and strong steps to sanction this type of abusive behavior.

13

TREATMENT OF VICTIMS AND PERPETRATORS

13.1 Burgess, Ann Wolbert
1985 "Sexual Victimization of Adolescents." Pp. 123-138 in Rape and Sexual Assault: A Research Handbook, edited by Ann Wolbert Burgess. New York: Garland.

Purpose: To provide a review of the literature sexual victimization of adolescents, including stranger rape, acquaintance rape, and incest and to examine the effects sexual victimization on developmental tasks of adolescents.
Method: Integrative review of literature.
Findings: Past research and National Crime Survey statistics on acquaintance rape are discussed. The author considers the impact that sexual victimization has on the adolescent developmental process. Any form of sexual victimization, it is concluded, can easily disrupt this process and produce serious effects in both the long and short run. Although the author concentrates on the crisis reactions to stranger assault, she notes that victims of acquaintance assault may experience similar symptoms and discusses the psychosocial impact of acquaintance assault on the victim. The impact on the adolescent includes psychological issues (an inability to feel protected by increasing defenses against the unknown and difficulty in attempting to make sense of what happened), social

issues (rapist and victim may continue to have interpersonal contact and a shared social group), and legal issues (an effect on the prosecution). Reactions of adolescents to non-stranger assault tend to be more variable than in cases of stranger assault. These findings may be a result of the many different types of assaults that are categorized together under the heading of "acquaintance rape."

13.2 Burgess, Ann Wolbert and Lynda Lytle Holmstrom
1974 Rape: Victims of Crisis. Bowie, MD: Robert J. Brady.

Purpose: The purpose of this book is to present a rape crisis counseling model developed by the authors. The information provided is intended not only for educating rape crisis counselors, but also for sensitizing others who deal with rape victims (such as medical and criminal justice professionals, family members, and friends) to the reality of rape as experienced by its victims.
Method: Clinical Experience
Findings: Included are descriptions of various types of rape, including rape by acquaintances and "confidence" rapes; a review of the consequences of rape, including Rape Trauma Syndrome; and information on rape crisis intervention and counseling.

13.3 Burkhart, Barry R.
1991 "Conceptual and Practical Analysis of Therapy for Acquaintance Rape Victims." Pp. 287-303 in Acquaintance Rape: The Hidden Crime, edited by Andrea Parrot and Laurie Bechhofer. New York: John Wiley and Sons.

Purpose: To discuss issues of treatment for victims of acquaintance rape and to develop a treatment protocol for such victims. Very little work has been done on this issue, so the literature to date is scant.
Method: Review of literature on acquaintance rape and other

forms of sexual exploitation.
Findings: Denial and delay of treatment are crucial characteristics of victimization by acquaintance rape. Recognition of these aspects is vital for successful treatment. Components of treatment are discussed with application to acquaintance rape.

13.4 Gidycz, Christine A. and Mary P. Koss
1991 "The Effects of Acquaintance Rape on the Female Victim." Pp.270-84 in Acquaintance Rape: The Hidden Crime, edited by Andrea Parrot and Laurie Bechhofer. New York: John Wiley and Sons.

Purpose: To review the unique aspects of the victimization experience for acquaintance rape. It is argued that victims of acquaintance rape may be at greater risk to experience negative behavioral, cognitive, and emotional consequences from their victimization, relative to the victims of other crimes due to the "pervasive, malevolent context of acquaintance rape."
Method: Review of literature and case study material.
Findings: Victims of acquaintance rape experience symptoms such as anxiety, depression, relationship and sexual difficulties, physical problems requiring medical attention, and changes in life style and behavior. While some of these symptoms are shared by victims of stranger rape, victims of acquaintance rape are much less likely to define what has happened to them as rape and they are less likely to seek professional help in dealing with their victimization. This makes the effects of their experience especially difficult and problematic in terms of long-term adjustment and recovery.

13.5 Katz, Bonnie L.
1991 "The Psychological Impact of Stranger versus Nonstranger Rape on Victim Recovery." Pp.251-69 in Acquaintance Rape: The Hidden Crime, edited by Andrea Parrot and Laurie Bechhofer. New York: John Wiley and Sons.

Purpose: To review the literature on the impact of prerape familiarity with the rapist on the recovery process for victims and to present the results of one particular study of whether there are important differences in the recovery process following rape by a stranger versus rape by someone familiar.
Method: Review of literature. The empirical data in the article come from a study of 87 women recruited from several rape crisis centers in the Washington, D.C. area. Data were collected by written, self-report questionnaires and in-person interviews.
Findings: The literature review shows little empirical work on the differences between stranger and acquaintance rape in terms of recovery. The work that has been done is inconsistent.

This particular empirical study indicates that there are clear differences. Women raped by an acquaintance (acquaintance, friend, intimate) attribute more blame to themselves, see themselves more negatively, and have higher distress than women raped by strangers. Stranger rapes tend to have a faster recovery process. The results should be used by clinicians and criminal justice personnel in their attempts to help victims of rape.

13.6 Kilpatrick, Dean G.; Connie L. Best; Benjamin E. Saunders; and Lois J. Veronen

1988 "Rape in Marriage and Dating Relationships: How Bad Is It for Mental Health?" In Human Sexual Aggression: Current Perspectives, edited by Robert A. Prentky and Vernon L. Quinsey. New York: Annals of the New York Academy of Sciences.

Purpose: The authors assert that rape by an acquaintance is just as traumatic as rape by a stranger, but that methodological problems have plagued previous work on the subject. The goal of the research is to improve upon previous studies of the differences in impact between the two types of rape.
Method: 43 adult victims of completed rape and 96 adult nonvictims were selected from a larger sample used for a National Institutes of Justice study of crime victimization and its

relationship to mental health. To qualify for the current study, victims had to have experienced no other serious crime victimizations, and nonvictims no crime victimizations at all. Subjects were contacted by telephone and then interviewed in-person about the rape experience (if any), possible mental health problems (using an instrument based on the Diagnostic Interview Schedule for the DSM-III), and current demographic characteristics.

Findings: Rape by a spouse or boyfriend was almost twice as common as rape by a stranger. Those raped by spouses or boyfriends were slightly (although not significantly) more likely than stranger rape victims both to experience injury and to fear being killed or seriously injured during the assault. Rape victims, as a group, manifested significantly higher rates of major depression, social phobia, and sexual dysfunction than the nonvictim group. Moreover, there were no differences between stranger and acquaintance rape victims in the frequency of these symptoms. The authors conclude that the identity of the offender does not affect the severity or likelihood of negative psychological outcomes for victims, and encourages greater public education on the subject to dispel the kinds of myths that further traumatize victims of acquaintance rape.

13.7 Koss, Mary and Barry Burkhart
1989 "A Conceptual Analysis of Rape Victimization: Long-Term Effects and Implications for Treatment." Psychology of Women Quarterly 13:27-40.

Purpose: To review the research on post-traumatic responses to rape. This article is relevant to acquaintance rape principally through the citation of the finding that many rape victims have been raped by a close acquaintance. Several case studies of acquaintance rape are cited as well in the discussion of long-term effects.

Method: Review of literature.

Findings: Cognitive adaptation and coping are particularly

important factors to examine in understanding long-term resolution of rape victimization and in providing clinical treatment for victims. There is a need for more research on the long-term cognitive-emotional responses to rape.

13.8 Koss, Mary P. and Mary R. Harvey
1991 The Rape Victim: Clinical and Community Interventions. Newbury Park: Sage.

Purpose: The authors' goal is to provide current, comprehensive information about rape for use by those who counsel and treat rape victims.
Method: Research Review
Findings: The authors describe the incidence and prevalence of rape, emphasizing that these may be underestimated in current "official" statistics. A community-based approach to understanding rape, including date rape on college campuses, is explored. Theory and models of the impact of rape are presented, and attention is also given to the consequences for male victims. Research on rape crisis centers is discussed, along with findings regarding clinical and group treatment strategies for victims. The authors conclude with a review of findings on primary and secondary rape prevention efforts.

13.9 Madigan, Lee and Nancy C. Gamble
1989 The Second Rape: Society's Continued Betrayal of the Victim. New York: Lexington Books.

Purpose: The purpose of this book is to expose what the authors refer to as the "second rape" of the sexual assault victim: the indifference of society and the frequent need of victims to change their own lifestyles in order to feel safe again.
Method: Research Review.
Findings: Different forms of rape, including rapes by acquaintances, are discussed via case histories of victims. Common experiences of victims with the police, doctors, the

criminal justice system and the mental health system are reviewed, with an emphasis on procedures and attitudes which may present difficulties for rape victims. Tips for coping with the "second rape" are presented, along with a feminist perspective on rape prevention which focuses on gender stratification.

13.10 Parrot, Andrea.
1989 "Acquaintance Rape Among Adolescents: Identifying Risk Groups and Intervention Strategies." Journal of Social Work and Human Sexuality 8:47-61.

Purpose: To discuss acquaintance rape by examining frequency, and characteristics of assaults, perpetrators, and victims. To provide advice for social workers who work with victims.
Method: Integrative review of literature
Findings: Characteristics of victims: Victims of acquaintance rape often, though not always, are female, have low self-esteem, external locus of control, follow traditional sex roles, have experienced previous sexual assault, and have a high status among their peer groups. Characteristics of perpetrators: Perpetrators generally do not know that their sexual assault was wrong. They often have low self-esteem, have been victimized in their past, follow traditional masculine sex roles, have other anti-social behavior, and want to improve status among their peers. Characteristics of assault: Three general stages of perpetrator behavior during acquaintance rape are discussed: (1) intimate behavior causing discomfort for a woman, (2) escalation of behavior and desensitization of victim, (3) forced intercourse in an isolated area. Counseling victims: Many victims will not label their assaults "rape" and may feel quilt or responsibility for the assault. Thus, social workers may find it difficult to identify victims. Victims who do not seek help often experience dysfunctional behavior patterns including: non-discriminating sexual behavior, withdrawal from social interaction, and repression of assault. Reaction of the first person that the victim discusses the assault with is vital for the recovery process. Social workers,

who are often in this role, should know the facts and local laws concerning acquaintance rape. Potential options for the victim are presented, but any decisions about reporting or discussing the assault should be made by the victim.

13.11 Parrot, Andrea
1991 "Medical Community Response to Acquaintance Rape Recommendations." Pp 304-16 in Acquaintance Rape: The Hidden Crime, edited by Andrea Parrot and Laurie Bechhofer. New York: John Wiley and Sons.

Purpose: To discuss the psychological and medical needs of acquaintance rape victims. To make recommendations for health care practitioners who deal with victims.
Method: Review of literature.
Findings: Issues of reporting, counseling needs, medical history taking, psychological responses of the victim, and the role of the health care practitioner are discussed. A summary list of suggestions is presented for use by health care practitioners to deal with the unique needs of acquaintance rape victims.

13.12 Rowan, Edward L. and Judith B. Rowen
1984 "Rape and the College Student: A Multiple Crisis in Late Adolescence." Pp. 234-250 in Victims of Sexual Aggression: Treatment of Children, Women, and Men, edited by Irving P. Stuart and Joanne G. Greer. New York: VanNostrand Reinhold.

Purpose: To discuss how the developmental tasks of adolescents can be applied to the stages of rape trauma to aid in treatment.
Method: Integrative review of literature
Findings: The authors discuss the five major tasks that the adolescent accomplishes while moving into adulthood: "(1) differentiation from parents with resolution of dependence issues,

(2) development of mature sexuality, (3) establishment of intimate relationships, (4) acquisition of a vocational role choice, and (5) clarification of a personal value system." These tasks of the developmental process can be used to develop a conceptual framework to use during psychotherapeutic intervention during the different stages of rape trauma, especially the acute, crisis phase and the resolution phase. These considerations are important for college campuses where the female student population is at a high risk for sexual assault.

14

PREVENTION PROGRAMS

14.1 Bachman, Ronet; Raymond Paternoster; and Sally Ward
1992 "The Rationality of Sexual Offending: Testing a Deterrence/Rational Choice Conception of Sexual Assault." Law and Society Review 26,2:343-372.

Purpose: To study the impact of social context, sanctions, and moral beliefs on the self-reported likelihood of committing sexual assault.

Method: The research used the factorial survey method. 94 male college students were presented with a set of five scenarios describing sexual assaults. They were asked a series of questions about each vignette, including how likely it was that they would act as the perpetrator did. Analysis of the results compared the likelihoods to variables describing the social characteristics of the assault, the perceived formal sanctions (e.g., dismissal from school, arrest), informal sanctions (e.g., social censure and loss of self-respect), and moral beliefs about the assault.

Findings: The results are generally supportive of deterrence research which finds a deterrent effect of sanctions. Perceived threat of formal sanctions did reduce the self-reported likelihood of committing sexual assault. However, informal sanctions had little effect. Moral beliefs were found to interact with formal sanctions; respondents who believed the vignette assaults were morally wrong were not affected by formal sanctions, but those who had low belief that the assault was morally wrong were more likely to respond to formal sanctions. Two of the social characteristics of the vignettes had significant effects; respondents were more likely to report they would commit an assault if the female had been partying or drinking, and if the female had willingly kissed and fondled the male prior to the assault. The authors conclude that deterring sexual assault among college males requires both moral education and formal sanctions against sexual assault.

14.2 Enke, Janet L. and Lori K. Suddekth
1991 "Educational Reforms." Pp. 149-160 in Sexual Coercion: A Sourcebook on Its Nature, Causes, and Prevention, edited by Elizabeth Grauerholz and Mary A. Koraleowski. Lexington, MA: Lexington Books.

Purpose: To review current educational programs concerned with sexual coercion and relate them to the context of primary and secondary schools. This is followed by a discussion of a multilevel comprehensive educational reform aimed at changing attitudes and preventing sexual coercion.
Method: Integrative review of literature.
Findings: Information about sexual assault and myths and attitudes about date rape are not generally part of the sex education curriculum in most primary and secondary schools. Programs, workshops, and manuals are available at the college level to alter attitudes and behaviors concerning sexual coercion. However, it is essential to start such programs early in the educational system before sexually coercive attitudes are formed. There has been some research that has found that, instead of ending sexual coercion, the educational system contributes to sexually coercive attitudes and behaviors. Practices such as gender segregation and extra curricular activities lead to norms of interaction which are centered on male power and female passivity and dependency which form the foundation for developing sexually coercive attitudes and behaviors. A multilevel, comprehensive approach to

reducing sexually coercive attitudes and behaviors is introduced. The program is aimed at children, adolescents, and young adults. It takes into account the social world of young people and the cultural environment of schools and seeks to empower students and to help them to develop into full men, women, and sexual beings. Healthier and broader definitions of sexuality and gender identification and information about sexual coercion are also included. Possible educational tools and potential barriers are discussed.

14.3 Levine-MacCombie, Joyce and Mary P. Koss
1986 "Acquaintance Rape: Effective Avoidance Strategies." Psychology of Women Quarterly 10:311-320.

Purpose: The goal of this study was to determine whether previous findings on the utility of various rape avoidance strategies could be replicated using a sample of only acquaintance rape victims, including any women who had had an experience that fit the legal definition of acquaintance rape (whether or not they acknowledged themselves to be rape victims).
Method: A survey, which included the Sexual Experiences Interview, was administered to a sample of 2,016 women (age 18-25) from a midwestern university, and in-depth interviews were conducted with 231 of these women.
Findings: Consistent with previous research on stranger rape, women who were able to avoid a potential acquaintance rape were less likely to have felt high levels of guilt and fear during the encounter, less likely to have perceived the encounter as violent, and more likely to have run away or screamed for help, than their victim counterparts. However, quarreling with the perpetrator was found to be more strongly related to rape completion than to avoidance. In contrast to findings regarding stranger rape, cognitive responses such as reasoning or crying were found to be effective strategies for avoiding acquaintance rape, but less so than the active strategies. Feeling anger and using physical resistance strategies during the assault were not significant predictors of

either rape completion or avoidance in this study. Unacknowledged victims of rape differed from acknowledged victims only in the combinations (not necessarily the types) of avoidance strategies they used.

14.4 Mann, Cynthia A.; Michael L. Hecht; and Kristen B. Valentine
1988 "Performance in a Social Context: Date Rape versus Date Right." Central States Speech Journal 39,3/4:269-280.

Purpose: The study examines the effects of trigger scripting in modifying sexual attitudes and preventing date rape. Trigger scripting "allows the researcher to explore the influence of performance through scripted and performed texts."
Method: Ninety-two undergraduate students participated in an experimental design where they were randomly assigned to one of four conditions: trigger scripting plus discussion, trigger scripting only, discussion only, and a control group. After the experimental condition, the subjects responded to a posttest that measured self reported assertive behavior, sexual attitudes, and experiences of sexual aggression. The trigger script, "Big Girls Don't Cry," depicted issues concerning assertiveness and dating by presenting information on how to prevent unwanted sexual aggression and date rape. The discussions were 15 minutes in length and focused on defining date rape and attitudes surrounding it.
Findings: The trigger scripting and discussion condition was the most effective condition overall, followed by the trigger scripting only condition. Both groups showed immediate changes in sexual attitudes in the posttest. In a follow-up survey, the trigger and discussion condition had the greatest effect on attitudes of those who had less aggressive sexual experiences.

14.5 McCormick, Naomi B.
1979 "Come-ons and Put-offs: Unmarried Students' Strategies for Having and Avoiding Sexual

Intercourse." Psychology of Women Quarterly 4,2:194-211.

Purpose: The objective of this study was to ascertain how college students would initiate or avoid sex on a date, and how they believe others would do so.
Method: 129 undergraduates completed a questionnaire including the Attitudes Towards Women Scale, two essay questions requiring subjects to explain what strategies they would use to initiate and to avoid having sex with a date, and a set of influencing and avoiding strategies for which students which asked to indicate what they believed to be the gender of the person using them.
Findings: Some subjects did not write down any influencing strategies in the essays; females were significantly more likely than males to be in this group, suggesting that women may be less likely to use influencing strategies. Males were more likely to report that they would use "direct" strategies (e.g logic, coercion) than females. Seduction was the modal strategy for subjects of both sexes. Women were more likely to use coercion and body language to avoid intercourse. Among both sexes, indirect strategies (e.g. body language, manipulation) were most often reported as a means of initiating sex, and direct strategies were most often reported to avoid sex. On the strategy-by-gender items, subjects associated all of the strategies for having sex with a man, and all strategies for avoiding sex with a woman; scores on the Attitudes Towards Women scale had no effect on these ratings. The findings suggest that there is a general belief that men are responsible for initiating sex, while women are responsible for avoiding it.

14.6 Muehlenhard, Charlene L. and Lisa C. Hollabaugh
1988 "Do Women Sometimes Say No When They Mean Yes? The Prevalence and Correlates of Women's Token Resistance to Sex." Journal of Personality and Social Psychology 54,5:872-879.

Purpose: The purpose of the study was to determine the

prevalence and characteristics of women who tell their dating partners that they do not want to have sex when, in fact, they are willing.

Method: Questionnaires were administered to 610 female undergraduates. Subjects were asked to estimate the number of times they had (1) said no to intercourse and meant no, (2) said no and meant maybe, (3) said no and meant yes. After each of these questions subjects chose from a list of possible reasons those which best explained their saying no. Subjects also completed the Sexual Opinion Survey which measures erotophobia-erotophilia, and five attitude scales: the Attitudes Toward Women Scale, the Adversarial Sexual Beliefs Scale, the Acceptance of Interpersonal Violence Scale, the Rape Myth Acceptance Scale, and the Sexual Beliefs Scale.

Findings: 39% of subjects reported saying no to sexual intercourse when they meant yes (token resistance). A factor analysis identified three groupings of reasons for this behavior: practicality (e.g. unsure of man's feelings), inhibitions (e.g. moral), and manipulative (e.g. wanting to make him wait). Subjects were divided into three groups: Group 1, sexually experienced women who had never used token resistance; Group 2, women who had used token resistance; and Group 3: sexually inexperienced women who had never used token resistance. Group 2 had more traditional attitudes about women than Group 1, but less so than Group 3. Group 2 subjects were less erotophobic than Group 3 subjects. Group 2 subjects scored highest on the Adversarial Sexual Beliefs and Acceptance of Interpersonal Violence Scales, and were more likely than other subjects to believe that women both use token resistance and want men to use force during sex.

14.7 Parrot, Andrea

1991 "Institutional Response: How can Acquaintance Rape be Prevented." Pp 355-67 in Acquaintance Rape: The Hidden Crime, edited by Andrea Parrot and Laurie Bechhofer. New York: John Wiley and Sons.

Purpose: To provide an overview of the steps necessary to college campuses to develop effective and successful acquaintance rape prevention programs.
Method: Review of literature and program material.
Findings: Many campuses are lagging in their efforts to develop prevention programs. Administrations need to acknowledge that the problem of acquaintance rape exists. Each campus should develop educational materials for students, faculty, and staff. Because of the link between acquaintance rape and alcohol, campuses need to confront alcohol use and to provide meaningful alternatives to the typical drinking party. Educational programs need to be designed that are campus-specific, that actively involve the students, and that are meaningful in terms of the experiences and interests of the students.

14.8 Parrot Andrea
1991 "Recommendations for College Policies and Procedures to Deal with Acquaintance Rape." Pp. 368-80 in Acquaintance Rape: The Hidden Crime, edited by Andrea Parrot and Laurie Bechhofer. New York: John Wiley and Sons.

Purpose: To provide recommendations for colleges about their policies dealing with acquaintance rape, their judicial processes, public safety, and services for victims.
Method: Review of literature and cases of acquaintance rape.
Findings: Detailed recommendations are provided for making revisions in campus policies and procedures. Policies should be clear, explicit, in written form, and readily available throughout campus. There should be a policy regarding unacceptable sexual behavior that clearly defines what is unacceptable and what the consequences will be for violations of that policy. The judicial process for dealing with problems should be similarly clear, explicit, and written down. The process should be followed closely in dealing with any cases of acquaintance rape. Services to support victims should be developed. These and other valuable recommendations are presented in this work.

14.9 Rozee, Patricia D.; Py Bateman; and Theresa Gilmore
1991 "The Personal Perspective of Acquaintance Rape Prevention: The Three-Tier Approach." Pp 337-54 in Acquaintance Rape: The Hidden Crime, edited by Andrea Parrot and Laurie Bechhofer. New York: John Wiley and Sons.

Purpose: To discuss strategies for rape prevention, with particular emphasis on acquaintance rape. Bateman's community-based prevention education work is the model for the discussion.
Method: Review of literature.
Findings: Rape prevention must be attacked on three levels or "tiers." The first is level of the society within which rape occurs. Cultural values and ideologies such as sexual entitlement, male supremacy, and acceptance of interpersonal violence can promote rape. They are reinforced by socialization patterns, and rape education programs can change these socialized attitudes. Changes in social institutions can also be a part of rape prevention programs. The second tier is "everyday life." This tier includes strategies women adopt to cope with the pervasive fear of rape. The stages of acquaintance rape are identified, and education programs need to communicate these to women so they can develop skills to deal with sexual coercion as they encounter it in their everyday lives. The third tier is labelled "confrontation," and it is at this level that women are dealing with an acquaintance rape situation. All three tiers should be included in comprehensive acquaintance rape prevention programs.

14.10 Wilson, Wayne and Robert Durrenberger
1982 "Comparison of Rape and Attempted Rape Victims." Psychological Reports 50: 198.

Purpose: The authors assessed differences between women who have successfully avoided rape and those who have not.
Method: Over a five-year period, a total of 447 female undergraduates were asked about their experience with rape and attempted rape. Subjects were surveyed in either a group or a

private setting, and answered questions about feelings of responsibility for the assault, how well they knew the offender, whether they had been drinking before the assault, whether the offender had been drinking before the assault, whether the offender apologized, and whether they dated the offender again.
Findings: The only variable which discriminated between victims and avoiders was whether they dated the offender again. Victims were more likely than avoiders to date the man again. Victims were also more likely to report multiple rape experiences. The authors suggest that victim's lifestyles and lack of understanding of men's sexual intent may explain some rapes.

14.11 Youn, Gahyun
1987 "On Using Public Media for the Prevention of Rape." Psychological Reports 61:237-238.

Purpose: This review paper advocates for rape prevention efforts.
Method: Research Review
Findings: Sex and sex role differences in attitudes towards rape result in a lack of cultural agreement as to what constitutes rape. For this reason, prevention efforts which address such differences may be more effective than legal reform. Mass media such as television would be a useful forum for acquaintance rape prevention information.

AUTHOR INDEX

SUBJECT INDEX

About the Compilers

SALLY K. WARD is Associate Professor of Sociology at the University of New Hampshire, where she has taught since 1980. Her areas of research include urban sociology and social policy, urban poverty and the underclass, family formation and childbearing, and acquaintance rape on college campuses.

JENNIFER DZIUBA-LEATHERMAN is a Doctoral Student in Sociology and a Project Assistant at the Family Research Laboratory at the University of New Hampshire. She has co-authored articles on child victimization, youth victimization prevention, and legal representation for children.

JANE GERARD STAPLETON is an Instructor in Women's Studies and Sociology at the University of New Hampshire. She is the former Coordinator of Direct Services for the Sexual Harassment and Rape Prevention Program. She speaks nationally on issues related to sexual violence.

CARRIE L. YODANIS is a Doctoral Student in Sociology at the University of New Hampshire. She is currently working on research in the areas of family violence, gender, and stratification.

HARDCOVER BAR CODE